DIRECTIONS IN DEVELOPMENT

The Political Economy of Democratic Decentralization

James Manor

The World Bank
Washington, D.C.

Library of Congress Cataloging-in-Publication Data

Manor, James
      The political economy of democratic decentralization / James
   Manor
          p.   cm. — (Directions in Development)
      Includes bibliographical references (p.   ) and index.
      ISBN 0-8213-4470-6
      1. Decentralization in government.   2. Economic
   development.   3. Democratization.   I. Title   II. Series:
   Directions in development (Washington, D.C.)
   JS113.M355   1999
   352.2'83—dc21   99-11245
                                                            CIP

POD by LSI

Contents

For Roderick MacFarquhar

Abstract

Nearly all countries worldwide are now experimenting with decentralization. Their motivations are diverse. Many countries are decentralizing because they believe this can help stimulate economic growth or reduce rural poverty, goals central government interventions have failed to achieve. Some countries see it as a way to strengthen civil society and deepen democracy. Some perceive it as a way to off-load expensive responsibilities onto lower level governments. Thus, decentralization is seen as a solution to many different kinds of problems.

This report examines the origins and implications decentralization from a political economy perspective, with a focus on its promise and limitations. It explores why countries have often chosen not to decentralize, even when evidence suggests that doing so would be in the interests of the government. It seeks to explain why since the early 1980s many countries have undertaken some form of decentralization.

This report also evaluates the evidence to understand where decentralization has considerable promise and where it does not. It identifies conditions needed for decentralization to succeed. It identifies the ways in which decentralization can promote rural development. And it names the goals which decentralization will probably not help achieve.

Foreword

Today over 80 percent of developing and transition countries of Eastern and Central Europe and the former Soviet Union, with widely different political orientations and economic bases, are experimenting with decentralization. This follows more than sixty years when the trend was to centralize power and resources. Central control had enabled governments to pull their economies out of the Great Depression and later to wage the Second World War. The strategy led to massive economic gains among industrial nations in the 1950s and 1960s, and to rapid economic growth and increasing world influence among Communist countries. Understandably, centralization became the model for development of the emerging nations in Africa, Latin America and Asia, reinforced by donor agencies including the World Bank.

However, the top-down approach has often failed to promote development and reduce poverty. Disappointment has been particularly high with rural development programs, many of which were initiated, designed and executed by central government representatives with little or no input from communities. To address these and other problems, starting in the mid-1980s, governments worldwide began decentralizing some responsibilities, decisionmaking authority and resources to intermediate and local governments and often to communities and the private sector.

This paper is a major contribution to our understanding of the decentralization movement and its implications for economic growth, poverty alleviation and the development of civil society and democratic institutions. It will be of interest to policymakers, development practitioners and scholars. The research was carried out as part of the World Bank's Decentralization, Fiscal Systems and Rural Development Research Program, supported by the Swiss Agency for Development Cooperation, the Royal Ministry of Foreign Affairs of the Government of Norway and the World Bank. The research program is a part of a major new initiative of the World Bank to revitalize rural development, essential to reduce poverty and increase food security without destroying the environment. This broad program is outlined in the strategy paper, *Rural Development: From Vision to Action* (World Bank, 1997b).

Ian Johnson, Vice President
Environmentally and Socially Sustainable Development Network

Acknowledgments

This study owes an immense debt to Hans Binswanger's searching questions and his encouragement to extend the enquiry well beyond its initial, limited concerns. Perceptive assistance from the World Bank team—Andrew Parker, Suzanne Piriou-Sall, Anwar Shah, Johan van Zyl, Wendy Ayres and others—was exceedingly valuable.

Insights from many people have been critically important—"critically" in more ways than one. They include Abdul Aziz, Joel Barkan, Harry Blair, Anand Inbanathan, Rene Lemarchand, David Leonard, S.S. Meenakshisundaram, Njuguna Ng'ethe, Leonardo Romeo, Paul Smoke, and Ole Therkildsen.

Collaborations with the United Nations Capital Development Fund, the Ford Foundation in India and Bangladesh, the Colombian Ministry of Rural Development, and the Swedish International Development Agency also enriched this work.

And crucially, Richard Crook did more than anyone to clarify my understanding of these issues. The support of the Department for International Development (formerly the British Overseas Development Administration) for our early research on this topic prepared the ground for this work.

James Manor, Brighton, June 10, 1998

Introduction

Decentralization has quietly become a fashion of our time. It is being considered or attempted in an astonishing diversity of developing and transitional countries (Dillinger, 1994)—by solvent and insolvent regimes, by democracies (both mature and emergent) and autocracies, by regimes making the transition to democracy and by others seeking to avoid that transition, by regimes with various colonial inheritances and by those with none. It is being attempted where civil society is strong, and where it is weak. It appeals to people of the left, the center and the right, and to groups which disagree with each other on a number of other issues.

Some policymakers and social scientists, influenced by neoliberal ideas, have viewed decentralization as a means of shifting power away from the commandist state which has discredited itself in their eyes through rent-seeking and other practices. Others, frustrated by the poor results of centrally organized interventions to reduce rural poverty, have begun to see decentralized mechanisms as a possible alternative. Enthusiasts for cooperative development efforts by village communities have viewed it as a means of encouraging this. Postmodernist anthropologists and a diversity of activists and commentators who stress the need to draw upon the knowledge of people at the grass roots see it as a means to that end. Advocates of pluralist, competitive politics have regarded decentralization as a device for deepening democracy or for prying closed systems open, to give interest groups space in which to organize, compete and otherwise assert themselves. Some politicians in central governments see it as a means of off-loading expensive tasks onto others lower down. The leaders of some substantially autocratic regimes in the South have seen it as a substitute for democratization at the national level, and as a safe way to acquire much-needed legitimacy and grass roots support. Taken together, these diverse groups represent a potent coalition for change.[1]

This study examines—from a political economy perspective—the origins of the current wave of decentralizations in less developed countries, and its implications—especially its promise and limitations for rural development. It is based mainly on empirical evidence drawn

1

from experiments with decentralization in a large number of countries. This evidence is imperfect and incomplete, but still extensive enough to tell us a great deal. It should be stressed, however, that the findings here may need to be revised after these experiments have more time to develop and make an impact—perhaps in areas where, at this early stage, they have achieved rather little. So the findings that appear here—even when they read like forceful assertions—are not intended as the final word on the subject.

The paper is divided into six parts. Part I defines terms, to show that the word "decentralization" can mean many different things. This study considers three types of decentralization: deconcentration or administrative decentralization, fiscal decentralization, and devolution or democratic decentralization. Each of these can occur in isolation, but any two (or all) of them can occur simultaneously. For reasons provided in Part I, this paper concentrates upon experiments with decentralization which (in varied ways) possess democratic content. Part I also notes the various *levels* to which power and resources are being decentralized—to the local level, or to one or more intermediate levels, or to both. It is important to recognize that the creation of a federal system by empowering regions is quite different from the empowerment of authorities at or near the grass roots. Mix the two, and you get something different yet again. This paper is therefore necessarily an assessment of varied decentralizations (plural), not decentralization (singular). The diversity of the phenomena under discussion here prevents this study from yielding the kind of clear, tidy findings some readers might desire.

Part II examines why political regimes have often tended not to decentralize, despite evidence that suggests doing so would facilitate development and serve regimes' interests—within limits. It identifies centralizing imperatives which are almost always at work, regardless of place or time. But it focuses on the leaders and governments that exercised power in the first generation or two after the World War II, when a belief in the utility of centralized modes of governance was widely shared. It then moves on to a later phase—the period between the mid-1970s and the early 1980s—during which centralization encountered major difficulties and doubts, but during which it was nonetheless often pursued more forcefully (or, if you like, desperately) than before.

Part III seeks to explain the tendency of many regimes during the period following the early 1980s—our main concern here—to decentralize. It assesses a number of conditions and forces which qualify as causes and some which do not. It then looks briefly at the mixed motives which often lay behind the decision to decentralize. Part III concludes by considering a body of work which helps—up to a point—to illuminate both the origins and the implications of decentralization.

Part IV examines the encounter between decentralized institutions and the environments in which they must operate. The focus here is on how politics and state-society relations impinge on these institutions, and vice versa.

Part V discusses the advantages and disadvantages (overwhelmingly the former) which attend decisions to decentralize to both the regional (or intermediate) level in a political system and to the local level, rather than to just one of these.

Part VI assesses the promise of decentralization for rural development. It is better equipped to achieve some things than others. Only if we understand this can we protect it from the disillusionment that will surely follow when expectations about its utility in certain areas are shown to be unrealistically high.[2]

Notes

1. See especially in this connection, the comments about an alliance (concerning the urban sector) of neoliberals, radical egalitarian reformers and technocrats in Latin America (Nickson, 1995, p. 14). Such alliances were less common in Asia and Africa, and in rural parts generally.

2. For readings that supplement the material presented on this point in Part IV of this paper, see Barrier, 1990 and 1991 (concerning decentralization mainly in the francophone Sahel region of West Africa); and Evers, 1994; Painter, 1991 and 1993; and Toulmin, 1994.

Part I
Defining Terms

L et us begin by considering some definitions of types of decentral-ization. We will then focus more intensely on forms of democratic decentralization, and conclude with a brief comment on the problem of levels to which decentralization can occur.

Types

Numerous definitions of "decentralization" emerge from the litera-ture. To keep this analysis manageable, the term here refers to changes which occur within political systems. This rules out three of six things which are sometimes discussed under this label.

The first type of change to be excluded is sometimes called "decen-tralization by default." This happens when government institutions become so ineffective that they fail almost entirely to make the influ-ence of central authorities penetrate down to lower level arenas, and people at the grass roots become heartily cynical about government. When this occurs in countries with lively civil societies, voluntary asso-ciations or nongovernmental organizations at lower levels sometimes step in to generate development projects. Resources for such projects—which are either mobilized at the local level or obtained from non-governmental sources higher up—accrue to these groups and a kind of "decentralization," unintended by government, takes place. We have only one well-documented case of this in the literature (Davis, Hulme, and Woodhouse, 1994), but there are no doubt other examples.[1] These are worthy of study—although they are far from problem-free—but since the present paper already faces a hugely complex task in analyz-ing other variants of decentralization—which are intended by govern-ments—we exclude them.

The second thing to be excluded is privatization—the handover of tasks formerly performed by state agencies to the private sector.[2] We omit it partly because it entails the transfer of tasks outside political systems and partly because the private sector firms which take them over (even from local authorities) are themselves often quite large

(World Bank, 1995). Therefore, privatization often involves a shift of power and resources from one major, centralized power center to another.

We also set aside one further type of decentralization, namely, "delegation"—of some responsibilities for development programs or projects to parastatal agencies. We exclude it, partly because it has only rarely been attempted and partly because when it has been tried, it has either failed to facilitate a genuine decentralization of decisionmaking or it has impeded project implementation, or both (Parker, 1995).

This leaves us with three key definitions. Following Parker's adaptation of Rondinelli's typology (Rondinelli, 1981; Parker, 1995), we can describe them as follows[3]:

a) Deconcentration or administrative decentralization,
b) Fiscal decentralization,
c) Devolution or democratic decentralization.

At times, two or all three of these types of decentralization occur simultaneously, but they can also occur in isolation.

The first of these, deconcentration, refers to the dispersal of agents of higher levels of government into lower level arenas. Parker describes it as "administrative decentralization," and these two terms will be used interchangeably here.

One point needs emphasis. When deconcentration occurs in isolation, or when it occurs together with fiscal decentralization but *without simultaneous democratization*—that is, when agents of higher levels of government move into lower level arenas but remain accountable only to persons higher up in the system—it enables central authority to penetrate more effectively into those arenas without increasing the influence of organized interests at those levels. The central government is not giving up any authority. It is simply relocating its officers at different levels or points in the national territory. In such circumstances, it tends in practice to constitute centralization, since it enhances the leverage of those at the apex of the system. This is especially true in less developed countries where ordinary people

> have small influence over any allocations in the modern sector, such as involve finance and the direction of skilled manpower. Their lack of knowledge excludes them from the affairs of government. This is particularly true of rural people, whose society and economy are still largely based on subsistence agriculture, and who are insulated from decisionmaking centers by poor communications. In this situa-

tion a "deconcentrated" field office takes most of its decisions—even major ones—without being subject to local pressures, though it may sometimes enter into voluntary consultations with local notables. Demands from central government are much stronger than those from the local population and the field officer (less secure than his counterpart in the West) is constantly concerned to satisfy his political masters" (Mawhood, 1993, pp. 2–3).

These themes are echoed in Olson (1971), Bates (1983) and Becker (1983 and 1985). A vivid example of this can be found in Moi's Kenya (Ng'ethe, 1993). (See also, Nellis, 1983; Rondinelli, 1981; and Oyugi, 1993.) When deconcentration produces, in effect, the opposite of decentralization, it hardly warrants consideration in this study. But it can also be linked to mechanisms which give people at lower levels some voice in the decisions made within state institutions, and in those cases it can produce a degree of genuine decentralization.

Second, the term decentralization sometimes refers to downward fiscal transfers, by which higher levels in a system cede influence over budgets and financial decisions to lower levels. This authority may pass to deconcentrated bureaucrats who are accountable only to superiors at higher levels, or to unelected appointees selected from higher up. That sort of arrangement is subject to the same concerns voiced by Mawhood in the quotation just above, although fiscal decentralization in isolation may be somewhat less prone to these tendencies than deconcentration. But since fiscal decentralization unattended by any steps towards democratization rarely increases the influence of organized interests at lower levels, this makes it difficult to regard it as an example of genuine decentralization. However, when such fiscal transfers are linked to mechanisms which give people at lower levels some voice, no one would describe it as anything other than decentralization.

Finally, there is devolution—the transfer of resources and power (and often, tasks) to lower level authorities which are largely or wholly independent of higher levels of government, and which are democratic in some way and to some degree.[4] (The problem of what qualifies as democratic is tackled in the section just below.)

This study concentrates on experiments with decentralization which entail some elements of devolution or democratization. It does so in part because this has been the main thrust of recent experiments with decentralization (Nickson, 1995) and because, as some World Bank analysts have recognized, "the decentralization of resources and responsibilities without...(democratizing) political reforms would have been incomplete and, probably, not conducive to socially effective results" (World Bank, 1995, pp. 2).

It does so because "There is no feasible substitute to an approach in which local governments, with the active participation of their communities, take the initiative and responsibility for the actions conducive to their institutional development" (World Bank, 1995, pp. 27). And because "Sustainable development of capacity at the local level is possible only when there is effective demand by local administrations and communities" (World Bank, 1995, pp. viii).

It is, at the least, exceedingly difficult for such demand to manifest itself unless some form of democratization has occurred along with deconcentration and/or fiscal decentralization. Anwar Shah has made similar comments in his work on fiscal decentralization (Shah, 1997).

To put the same point differently, we will see in this study that greater accountability of government institutions—the most crucial element in successful decentralizations (Crook and Manor, 1994)—can be hard to obtain *even when substantial democratic elements are introduced into the decentralizing process*. When they are absent, or when reforms entail only minimal steps towards democratization, the impediments to greater accountability tend to be well nigh insurmountable.

The insistence here upon the need for democratic content if decentralization is to possess much promise should not, however, blind us to one further, important reality: devolution or democratic decentralization on its own is likely to fail. Democratic authorities at lower levels in political systems will founder if they lack powers and resources— meaning both financial resources and the administrative resources to implement development projects (see Part IV). In other words, decentralization must be attended both by some fiscal decentralization (since that supplies financial resources) and by some deconcentration or administrative decentralization (since that supplies bureaucratic resources required for implementation). If it is to have significant promise, decentralization must entail a mixture of all three types: democratic, fiscal and administrative.[5] So throughout this study, when reference is made to decentralization which offers some promise, the presumption is that such a tripartite mixture exists. The assertion in the *World Development Report 1997* that such tripartite mixtures rarely occur is erroneous—they are reasonably common[6] (World Bank, 1997a, p. 121).

One last, modest comment is in order here. Decentralization is almost always the result of intentional decisions by policymakers. But there is such a thing as inadvertent decentralization. This is not the same as decentralization by default, mentioned above. It occurs when other policy innovations produce an unintended decentralization of power and resources as a by-product. Two main examples come to mind—a small number, but they have occurred in large, important countries. The first is Russia, where authorities at lower levels have acquired greater powers than the central authorities intended as a result of oversights and unexpected developments (Gibson and Hanson, 1996). The second is China, where provincial governments have obtained more resources (and power over them) than central leaders wished. These examples of inadvertence are not excluded from this discussion, but the emphasis here will be on intentional attempts at decentralization.

Forms of Democratic Decentralization

Democratic decentralization can take varied forms. It clearly includes cases in which the persons in authority within institutions at intermediate or local levels are elected by secret ballots.[7] Elections may be direct or indirect—in the latter case, elected representatives at lower levels select members or higher level authorities. The persons who are elected may be the members of a council, or the executive head of an authority, or both. Elections are usually on a "first-past-the-post" basis, but they sometimes make use of some form of proportional representation.

All such cases qualify as examples of "democratic decentralization," but we need to avoid the narrow view that no set of arrangements other than these is admissible.[8] We should, for example, accept systems—often seen in francophone countries—where competing political parties put forward lists of candidates for seats on an authority, with the party that gains the most votes becoming the only party represented therein. Francophone systems also often permit the heads of such authorities to hold positions in national-level parliaments and cabinets—in accordance with the principle of *cumul des mandats* (the accumulation of mandates).[9] Such systems may be less healthy for the democratic process than those more familiar in the English-speaking world. Losing parties that are utterly excluded from power in this winner-take-all game may feel deeply aggrieved, so that the legitimacy of such institutions suffers. And heads of decentralized bodies who are also active at the national level may be preoccupied with high politics, and thus less responsive to popular pressure from lower levels. But it would be unhelpful to exclude these systems here.

We also need to include certain other, unconventional arrangements. In the Philippines, nongovernmental organizations have officially been given voting powers on local councils (Brillantes, 1994). In Colombia, we encounter local level "construction projects...that involve community contributions in labor, materials or cash, and *for which there is community supervision*" (World Bank, 1995, p. 6). The italics (which I have added) identify the critical element here. Community contributions which provide people with no voice cannot be regarded as democratic, but when some form of supervision or influence is permitted, they have some democratic content.

Such supervision or influence over projects or decisions by local authorities is often informal—which is to say that it is not well-institutionalized (World Bank, 1995). This is a less than fully reliable means of rendering systems democratic, since it often depends on the goodwill of local office holders, some of whom may prefer to avoid it. This is worth stressing here, because some important World Bank documents (for example, World Bank, 1995, pp. 73–79) appear to reveal a preoccupation with this sort of involvement of local people in development project cycles, rather than with the promotion of well-established, elected institutions (Blair, 1995, p. 8).

Nevertheless, when such participatory arrangements exist, they inject some democratic content into the system. We also need to accept other devices which provide people at the local level with some influence. These include efforts by local authorities to seek information on community needs and ways of addressing them, to establish local committees whose purpose is to foster active community participation, to organize and coordinate community involvement in projects (sometimes by hiring private firms to promote this), and to organize disenfranchised groups in order to assist them in voicing demands (which is sometimes done by central government agencies) (World Bank, 1995, pp. 14–15 and 23).

These devices are usually used by *elected* local authorities, but even in (the quite rare) cases where this occurs in the absence of elections, it is possible to say that a democratic element is—at least tenuously—present. Finally, we should recognize that occasions where authorities seek to draw community leaders and voluntary associations into consultations and decisions about development can—if they are not cynical exercises to give the appearance of openness before a government's initial intentions are implemented—bring at least a minimal degree of democracy into a system.

There are, of course, arrangements which appear democratic but amount to deceptions. For example, a system in which voters queue up to be counted behind symbols of their preferred candidates—used in the Nigerian local elections in March 1996—is open to abuse and must be regarded as extremely dubious. And where unconventional devices amount only to half-measures, they need to be identified as such. But half-measures are better than none at all, and sometimes they permit people at the local level to begin to pry systems open in ways that those in authority did not anticipate.

Levels

To complicate matters further, decentralization can entail transfers of power to different levels within political systems. It can be bestowed on one or more intermediate levels (regions and/or subregions). When this involves the creation of fully blown governments at the regional level, it qualifies as federalism. But more limited powers may go to intermediate levels, in experiments which fall short of outright federal restructuring.

Other experiments entail transfers to the local level, or to arenas quite close to it. We need to recognize that there is a difference between experiments which empower intermediate levels and those that empower local levels. That may sound obvious, but some analysts fail to grasp it.[10] And of course, some experiments entail simultaneous transfers to one or more intermediate levels *and* to local levels. (Such arrangements, about which questions often arise from policymakers, are discussed in detail in Part V.)

This is not a short document, but even in a study of this length, it is impossible to provide a comprehensive analysis of all of the permutations that flow from the various types of decentralization listed above (and mixtures thereof in variegated sequences—see Part IV below), plus the various levels to which transfers occur. Nor can we begin to exhaust the complex implications which arise from variations in the size of the national political arenas within which decentralization takes place. Decentralization in Botswana is bound to mean something different from decentralization in India. We can go quite a long way in this discussion despite this limitation, but readers should still be aware of it.

Readers will also notice that some of the experiments with decentralization discussed here are wholly or substantially located in urban areas.[11] This may seem odd, since this study deals with the utility of decentralization for rural development. But some urban initiatives carry useful lessons that have general application, and where that is true, they are considered here.

One last comment is in order here. *The World Development Report 1997*, in its excessively economistic discussion of decentralization, stresses the benefits that allegedly follow from "competition between levels of government" (World Bank, 1997a, p. 122). It will become apparent—particularly from Part IV of this study—that the main gains arise not from competition, but from cooperation between levels in decentralized systems.

Notes

1. Research on nongovernmental organizations in the Gambia (the country studied in the paper) indicates that their effectiveness is hindered by resource dependence and organizational weakness. They are seriously limited in their ability to complement government development programs—much less replace them. There is also a tendency for nongovernmental organizations there to duplicate efforts in certain fields and to omit others from their activities. Coordination of their efforts has been sadly lacking. (I am grateful to Ann Hudock for this information.) So there is reason to doubt whether "decentralization by default" offers a helpful alternative to conventional government efforts.

2. Bennett, 1990 and Bennett, 1994 ably analyze this.

3. There are good arguments for staying with Rondinelli's original formulations. I have chosen Parker's here mainly in the interests of consistency with other studies that parallel this one.

4. These authorities do not always have to be created anew. For example, in Latin America after May 1994, municipal mayors who had previously been appointed (and who had thus been agents of the central authorities) were "freely elected in every country except Cuba and Haiti" (Nickson, 1995, p. 2). This might be regarded as democratization rather than democratic decentralization. But since the new mayors were no longer agents of national governments, this change represented a de facto transfer of power from the national governments to the local level—it entailed both democratization and decentralization.

5. I am grateful to Suzanne Piriou-Sall for putting the point to me in these terms.

6. Such tripartite systems often develop when fiscal and democratic decentralizations occur to levels at which administrative decentralization has already taken place.

7. Indeed, we can go further and say that it also ought to entail "the elimination of exclusionary political practices, including fraud, unfair limits on voter registration,...the lack of ballot secrecy, voter intimidation, and vote buying" (Fox, 1994, p. 106). But this discussion is less about what ought to be than what is admissible under the label of democratic decentralization. Very limited infringements of the standards set out in the quotation above—for example, in vote buying, a widespread practice—should not cause us to exclude a system from consideration under this label.

8. This offers a contrast to the narrower definition adopted in some other studies—for example, Blair (1995).

9. See for example, the communes of Côte d'Ivoire assessed in Crook and Manor, 1994.

10. This failure is very common among people who study China—not least because the Chinese themselves make a habit of using the word local to refer to provincial and other intermediate levels—but it also arises in studies of some other countries. See for example, Fabian and Straussman (1994) on Hungary.

11. Indeed, there is a discernible shift of emphasis by some development agencies such as United States Agency for International Development towards decentralization in urban areas (Blair, 1995).

Part II
The Problem of Hubris: Regimes' Centralizing Tendencies and Earlier Experiments with Decentralization

A word of warning is in order. Most of the discussion here and in Part III which follows is inevitably pitched at a high level of generality, since we are seeking to extract insights of a general kind from a huge number of diverse cases. As a result, this study may irritate social scientists who have an appetite for analytical rigor. Historians, whose craft this account follows, will also feel disgruntled because it has been written so soon after the events which it assesses. This writer shares these misgivings, but to understand the origins of the recent wave of decentralizations, we need to attempt this sort of analysis.

Part II tackles one central question: Why have governments in developing countries tended (at least until recently) to centralize fiscal and decisionmaking power in ways that entail rural disempowerment? Part of the answer is provided by a tendency which can be observed in nearly all times and places, including the present—the fashion for decentralization notwithstanding. Politicians everywhere strive to enhance their power, and those who stand at the apex of any political system therefore tend toward centralization.

The trouble with this comment is that it barely gets us over the threshold of our analysis. It ignores a growing number of cases in which high-level leaders have grasped the subtlety that bargains with people at lower levels (bargains which require some decentralization of power and resources) often make their influence penetrate downward more effectively. More crucially, this generalization about the centralizing habit of most high-level politicians at most times can distract us from the special and more specific reasons for the centralization that occurred during the first generation or two after the Second World War.

The Age of Hubris

Let us begin by looking at the leaders of the industrialized nations in that period, whose views came to be widely shared by their counterparts in developing parts of the world. All of the governments which prosecuted World War II had to centralize power and resources, and "in close collaboration with large-scale industry and the unions, carried on a war economy with spectacular results" (de Swaan, 1988, p. 223). Those which were on the winning side naturally emerged from the conflict with great faith in the efficacy of commandist modes of governance. And of course, even before the war, centralization had helped many regimes to cope with the consequences of the depression. So leaders in that generation tended strongly towards both centralization and the concentration of substantial power in the public sector. This was true not only of regimes in the Soviet bloc, but of most other governments too. Where Leninist principles were rejected, Keynesian approaches usually predominated.

This belief in the centralized state was bolstered by the spectacular advances during the 1950s and 1960s of economies which were managed along both Keynesian and Leninist lines.

> World output of manufactures quadrupled between the early 1950s and the early 1970s and, what is even more impressive, world trade in manufactured products grew tenfold...world agricultural output also shot up, if not so spectacularly (Hobsbawm, 1994).

Keynesian managers of national economies in the West believed that they had ways of avoiding the boom and bust cycles that had long bedeviled capitalism.

> Capitalism had been reformed out of all recognition [thanks to the enlarged role for centralized states]. Despite occasional minor recessions and balance of payments crises, full employment and at least a tolerable degree of stability are likely to be maintained (Crosland, 1956, p. 517).

For over two decades after the Second World War, Western leaders tended to believe in the idea of progress—based in part on the assumptions that the resources of the planet were inexhaustible, and that science and technology would ensure their availability to all[1]—and in mixed economies guided by centralized economic management from the government side (Hobsbawm, 1994). "The war economy had reconciled big business with government intervention" (de Swaan, 1988, p. 224), and the postwar boom sustained this.

One important development which reinforced this faith in the utility of centralized governance was the unprecedented postwar expansion of public services and welfare state provisions in Western Europe and North America. It was widely believed that in periods when growth slowed, these arrangements would ease the distress felt by vulnerable groups. There was every confidence that slowdowns would not be prolonged, that the economic boom would prevail and make it possible to fund welfare provisions, and that the state apparatus had the capacity to implement them.

The experiences of wartime military administration, production battles, civil protection of evacuation schemes and propaganda campaigns had taught Western governments how to steer the economy, to orchestrate public opinion and to manage the lives of their citizens to a degree that seemed to dwarf the demands of running a welfare state, a task which not so long ago had seemed so formidable (de Swaan, 1988, p. 224).

There is reason to doubt whether the performance of many governments in constructing and managing their war efforts was quite so impressive as popular and elite memories of this process suggested. One good journalist, assessing the imperfections that attended America's preparations for war that he witnessed, notes that the cost was counted "in the coin of delay, confusion and waste."

> In the end, the preparations for war succeeded only because the country had manpower, skill, resources and industrial capacity enormous enough to succeed in spite of itself. And because a nation coming out of ten years of deep depression had a great pool of men and women who had been unemployed for so long that they were hungry for jobs and eager to work anywhere, anytime, doing anything. And because the government applied to the civilian economy the old philosophy of the U.S. Army—if enough men and weapons are poured into a confused battle situation, an enemy can be overwhelmed rather than defeated; and if masses of manpower and equipment are sent in, the probability is that sooner of later, by the grace of God, somebody will do something right (Brinkley, 1996, p. 52).

But victory in war largely erased memories of such shortcomings, so that most people clung firmly to the belief that centralized governance had great virtue and promise.

Those production battles, evacuation schemes and the prosecution of military campaigns more generally had, especially in the United States, persuaded key elites of the utility of a new set of techniques that had begun to emerge before the war. They dealt with the collection, manipulation and interpretation of quantitative data in ways that appeared to provide policymakers atop centralized systems with something like "scientific" management tools with great predictive power. It took time for these techniques to become known and to command widespread confidence. But by the early 1960s, the emergence of Robert McNamara as United States Secretary of Defense fostered a widespread belief in them, at least for a time (Hendrickson, 1996).

This—and, more crucially, the economic boom and the successful creation and operation of new social welfare systems, which were widely popular—confirmed the belief in the efficacy of centralized, commandist approaches to governance. Indeed, that belief enjoyed greater currency during the period after the Second World War than at any time in modern history.[2] The Organisation of Economic Co-operation and Development, as the voice of the consensus among its member nations, retained a firm faith in the benefits of centrally managed mixed economies well into the 1970s.

This outlook was naturally transmitted to many regimes in Latin America, Africa and Asia—including the newly independent nations on the latter two continents. One authority on African politics, looking back at the widespread belief in centralized governance, sees "hubris resonating throughout the world" in those years (Young, 1994, p. 3).

In the emerging nations of Africa and Asia, there were additional reasons for the popularity of such ideas. Close state regulation of economies in those countries, which had its origins in wartime controls imposed by colonial powers to support the war effort, were now taken over by successor regimes to ensure the optimal utilization of scarce resources such as capital and foreign exchange (see for example, Nayar 1997). In the waning years of empire, the old colonial regimes—facing serious challenges to their legitimacy and wishing to portray decolonization as a kind of fulfilment—had also tended to embark energetically (if belatedly) on development. In the postwar years, that word became "a master concept in world affairs" (Young, 1994, p. 211).

The efforts to make it manifest were assisted by highly favorable economic conditions: "booming commodity prices, metropolitan public capital, swelling domestic resources." The 1950s in colonial Africa became "a decade of broadly shared increase in well-being, probably the sole such extended period of the colonial age." In most of the remaining colonies, "plans" were adopted, cataloguing public investment aspirations as texts of prospective developmental accomplishment (Young 1994, pp. 211–12). The world witnessed what John Hargreaves has called "a 'second colonial invasion' in the form of a large-scale infusion of technical experts" (Hargreaves, 1979, p. 41, quoted in Young, 1994, p. 212). Welfare infrastructures burgeoned, by now almost universally desired and mirroring the development of the welfare states in the metropolis...the school and the clinic...safe drinking water, access roads, public housing." (Young, 1994, p. 212).

The economic boom of the 1950s "translated into a spectacular expansion in revenue flows." State expenditure increased elevenfold in the Belgian Congo between 1939 and 1950; and tenfold in the Gold Coast/Ghana between 1950 and 1960 and in Nigeria between 1937 and 1957; more than tenfold in Senegal and Côte d'Ivoire between 1946 and 1955, and fifteenfold in Guinea in the same period (Young, 1994, pp. 213–15). Not surprisingly,

> there began a dynamic expansion of the state apparatus, supported by the revenue revolution, that was carried forward and accelerated in the first two decades of independence [in Africa]. The developmentalist, welfare state of the terminal period was an apparatus very different from the minimalist vehicle of alien hegemony of the earlier phases (Young, 1994, pp. 214–15).

Nor was this merely a matter of economics. There were political and psychological dimensions to it as well. The new regimes that emerged in the ex-colonies were—quite naturally—*more* commandist than those in Europe, for two main reasons. After all, the former imperial powers had been more commandist in their colonies than they were at home.

> The now profoundly rooted hegemonical habits of the colonial state had produced in Africa [and Asia] a more hybrid capitalist order, where the postulates of a market economy became interwoven with the political reflexes of action by command..."Development" was a managerial art; the role of the administrator was the "encadrement" of the populace, to secure compliance with the edicts through which development policy was translated into administrative law (Young, 1994, pp. 215 and 286–87).

Most of the new ruling parties in these ex-colonies had also just succeeded in what were usually highly centralized campaigns for self-rule. In some cases, this had entailed a considerable struggle. In others, it was achieved with ease—the WASPy journalist James Cameron wrote of Lee Kwan Yew waging the struggle for independence on the golf courses of Singapore. But in every case—especially where self-government had come easily—these triumphs naturally inclined the new leaders to the view that further great accomplishments were likely, if they could sustain unified efforts by centralized, homogenizing means.

And there was so much to be done. Historians, especially those whose study Africa, have repeatedly stressed that during the colonial era, economies

> were deliberately structured on the basis of favoritism toward the export sector. Production of exportable commodities was emphasized so that the earnings from these commodities could be used to import manufactured goods from European metropoles. Industry was either neglected altogether or was emphasized only insofar as it contributed to the export sector, for instance, in the preliminary processing and packaging of primary exports (Lofchie, 1994, pp. 157–58).

After independence, the leaders of new nations facing these problems felt compelled to develop more diversified industrial sectors, and sometimes to attend to the interests of rural groups who had gained less than they might from the old arrangements. To achieve that, centralized approaches to the management of their economies seemed necessary.

Merilee Grindle has argued that in the immediate postindependence period, those leaders usually had the popularity to act as "relatively autonomous" agents, free from the trammels of preexisting interests (1989, p. 38). This is an important point, since it raises doubts about the writings of Robert Bates, Eliot Berg, and Michael Lipton on the direction of causality in that period. In their view, the policies which politicians adopted were driven by preexisting interests to which leaders were beholden. Grindle and Michael Lofchie, however, look at things the other way round. They argue persuasively that "the policies that African leaders adopted in many cases gave rise to interest groups that then came to demand the perpetuation and enlargement of the policy framework" (Lofchie, 1994, p. 157).

Once such interests crystallized and applied pressure on national leaders, commandism became more difficult, which is one of the reasons it eventually fell from favor. But for a time, it was quite feasible in most countries, and even when it became less practicable as interests asserted themselves, the commandist habit among politicians died hard, as we shall see.

The leaders of newly independent nations also saw large-scale development projects as a matter of urgency. Services—education, health care, basic sanitation—on which the quality of life and even the survival of ordinary people often depended were badly needed. So were socioeconomic reforms—in, for example, inequitable patterns of land control—which the colonial regimes had often neglected. Since many of these countries were rather artificial creations of European powers, centralized rule was also seen to be essential to prevent internal diversity from fragmenting the new nations. The provision of these things—especially services and reforms—was often seen not just as a political and economic necessity, but as a *moral* obligation of emergent central governments. This naturally persuaded the leaders of these new regimes of the *nobility*, the *righteousness* of commandist approaches to governance.

Local or regional councils, which some colonial authorities had created, might be maintained or occasionally extended in the name of deepening democracy. But they were often held in low esteem by the new rulers because they had been used by the imperial powers as mere sops and substitutes for self-determination at the national level. In such circumstances, it was hardly surprising that national consolidation through centralized leadership should receive greater emphasis.

This tendency was reinforced by faith in modern technology which both centralized states and many large private enterprises brought into play. This had threatening implications for decentralized institutions. Recent research on India in the 1950s gives us access to perhaps the most telling case in point. In the early years after Indian independence in 1947, the Gandhian vision of local-level self-sufficiency coexisted uneasily but tolerably well with the Nehruvian vision of rapid development led by a centralized state deploying high technology. The Community Development Programme, created in that period, sought to draw democratically self-governing local communities into partnership with the centralized state in a drive for rural development.

And yet when India experienced food shortages in those years, pressure began to build from the U.S. Agency for International Development, the Ford Foundation and other agencies to pursue more centralized, technology-led approaches to rural development. The criteria by which progress in such development was officially measured were altered. The contributions of local bodies pursuing microlevel projects were deemphasized, in favor of methods which used the latest technology and fixed more firmly on large-scale achievements of centralized programs. This, together with the desire of state-level legislators in India's federal system to claw back powers that had been decentralized, led gradually to the demise of the Community Development Programme.[3]

The situation which emerged in postindependence Africa in and after the 1960s has been described rather differently, but the same basic message comes through. In countries which had decentralized authorities, national leaders found themselves with

> the *negative* power to prevent (those authorities)...from taking independent initiatives, but not the positive power to implement policies that would improve social welfare. The central government's control became considerably more "inelastic," because state officials chose to rely on tools of coercion instead of techniques of persuasion (Kasfir, 1993, p. 25).

Before independence in Africa, decentralization had provided nationalist movements with leverage in the struggle for self-rule. But thereafter,

> ...it not only became irrelevant, it retained the threatening potential of support for opposition parties which had not succeeded in winning national power...to threaten the new governments in the same way that they had harassed the colonial authorities (Kasfir, 1993, p. 30).

Nor did Africa's decentralized institutions distinguish themselves in ways that might have earned them reprieves.

> Almost every council in southern Nigeria and Sierra Leone was dissolved at one time or another *before* the military *coups d'etat* began. The Kenyan Minister of Local Government...[referred to councils'] "incompetence, dereliction of duty, failure to collect revenue, failure to keep accounts [and] failure to maintain financial control" (Kasfir 1993, p. 34).[4]

To make matters worse, "the brevity of the colonial experience with democracy in general and decentralization in particular provided little time for the habit of political participation...to become deeply ingrained." And "the absence of norms preventing the elimination of opponents from the political arena" (Kasfir, 1993, p. 32), meant that whatever promise decentralized institutions had was smothered.

Commandist leaders throughout most of the South gave decentralized authorities little chance to achieve things, and this set up a vicious circle. Without adequate powers and resources, decentralized bodies accomplished little. This made everyone—people at the grass roots and national leaders—less inclined than ever to believe in the potential of decentralization, and that impelled leaders to centralize still further.

Commandist thinking was reinforced in that period by the prestige which the Soviet system enjoyed in some new nations—not just in Communist countries, but in India and parts of Latin America and sub-Saharan Africa. Numerous leaders hoped to replicate the USSR's rapid industrialization and were further encouraged by evidence during (though not after) the 1950s that the Soviet bloc economies were growing faster than their Western counterparts (Hobsbawm, 1994).

Since many of the emerging Asian and African leaders seemed heroic figures after years in opposition to foreign rule, it was easy for people to trust and even to revere them, to share the leaders belief in the moral rectitude of commandist governance. Ordinary folk worried far less than they do today about ensuring that politicians be held accountable for their actions. Faith in these leaders—who seemed more inspiring than prominent figures in the private sector—translated easily into faith in the concentration of state power over which they presided.

It also needs to be recognized that centralized governance *did* manage some significant achievements—or what passed as such—in that early phase. National unification of a sort was realized in most of these countries. India made substantial strides towards industrialization led by the state, a new and workable constitutional order came into being, and state boundaries were rationalized along linguistic lines without threatening national unity. Before the excesses of the Great Leap Forward, the Chinese mainland witnessed a significant redistribution of resources and the creation of institutions that secured national unity and provided basic education and health care. And so it went on across much of Asia. Latin American regimes tended to cling to their centralist traditions, and in the midst of the postwar economic boom, it was easy for most of them to appear capable of at least some achievements. In Africa, where European rule persisted longer, people had high hopes about the promise of centralized rule after independence (Moris, 1972). As a consequence: "Until the late 1980s, decentralization experiments in sub-Saharan Africa tended in the majority of states to reinforce central control rather than enhance local autonomy" (Tordoff, 1994, p. 555).

In that era, donor agencies—including even the U.S. Agency for International Development, despite American hesitations about socialism—were eager to deal with centralized state agencies in the third world, because they could "get things done quickly" (Nickson, 1995, p. 6). And the *big* things which they could get done—dams, port facilities, large hospitals, and others—were the kinds of things which the donors then preferred. In the confident atmosphere that prevailed from the end of the war through the 1960s, this preference for giantism was understandable. Then as now, achievements in small, scattered arenas were much harder for aid agencies to dramatize to taxpayers and legislatures in the West who were funding aid programs.

At least a small part in this centralizing story was played by the two paradigms that dominated the study of third world politics until the early 1970s or so—the "political development/modernization" approach and dependency theory. Both can be—and usually were—interpreted in ways that inclined regimes to centralize power and resources. The richest study to emerge from the political development school, Samuel P. Huntington's *Political Order in Changing Societies* (1968), is a subtle and complex work that is open to varied interpretations. But the tendency was to read (or misread) it as an argument for centralization—as a case for maintaining strong central authority capable of preventing civil society from becoming so disruptive that it threatened "political order." Dependency theory tended to be a source of encouragement for leftist or center-leftist statism and for siege economies.

It should also be remembered that patronage systems which evolved in some less developed countries actually *worked* after a fashion (or appeared to) in those years. This was partly due to the contrast with what had gone before. Most of these systems—no matter how limited their reach—were improvements on what had existed during the colonial era.

Patronage systems varied considerably in their breadth of impact. Many delivered the lion's share of resources to quite limited numbers of clients with immediate access to senior politicians. Those clients sometimes distributed spoils still further among their backers, but this usually failed to occur very effectively. A smaller number of patronage systems were less personalized and more institutionalized, and this ensured that a much wider array of interests received at least some resources.

The most impressive examples of this were probably the political machines which India's Congress Party developed at the state level in that federal system. In the first 15 to 20 years after independence in 1947, that party's organization was sufficiently extensive and disciplined to channel enough goods and services to enough interest groups (or elites within them) to guarantee that the Congress would gain legislative majorities in free elections against a divided opposition. This ensured Congress dominance at both state and national level for a remarkably long time. But this case was the exception rather than the rule.

In those early years, patronage systems (and centralized systems of governance more generally) suffered little from five problems which eventually overtook them. First, the demand for benefits from governments had yet to outstrip their capacity to respond. Second, slow (or no) economic growth had not yet taken a heavy toll on that capacity. Third, within some of those systems, middle-level political activists had not yet begun pocketing huge proportions of the resources passed to them. Fourth, senior leaders in many nations had not yet gone to excess in centralizing power in ways that eroded the institutional strength and autonomy of many of these systems. Finally, ordinary people had not yet experienced a severe loss of faith in the first generation of national leaders, or in their successors who often seemed less heroic and charismatic.

The Unraveling

Before long, however, all of these things began to happen—unevenly and to different degrees in different countries. At the core of the change stood a resource crunch—although, as we shall see, there was much more to it than that. "Revenue requirements of the postcolonial state were sharply higher" (Young, 1994, pp. 211). And the trends which emerged amid prosperity in the 1950s and 1960s "became a liability in the postcolonial states from the 1970s on, when economies turned sour..." (Young, 1994, pp. 287).

Commandist management of less developed economies which had initially made sense—by helping to manage and marshal scarce resources and to promote the development of sectors of economies whose growth had been stunted in the colonial era—now served to hold those very sectors back. It undermined their capacity to adapt to new conditions, especially amid recession in and after the mid-1970s (see for example, Nayar, 1997, pp. 29-33). Regimes found themselves trapped in "path dependency" (North, 1990), and it proved exceedingly difficult to throw off old, time-honoured habits of mind.

Confidence in centralized approaches to the management of national economies was shaken, in the late 1960s and early 1970s, when it became clear that stagflation could occur in the United States. It had been happening in developing countries—especially in Latin America—for a decade or so before that, but its emergence in the most potent of all economies made it impossible to ignore. This was largely unanticipated in prevailing economic theories. At first, it was argued that normality would soon reassert itself, and that tradeoffs between inflation and unemployment would become available once again. But when this stubbornly failed to occur, major doubts arose about the economic orthodoxy of the time.[5]

The resource crunch and material forces did not, however, determine outcomes in this period. It is worth stressing this point—which looms large here and in Part III—given the serious overstatement in the *World Development Report 1997*, that "Since the early 1980s, economic crisis has been by far the most important factor driving the introduction of ambitious reforms" (World Bank, 1997a, p. 151). That may be true of some reforms, but where decentralization is concerned, the story is much more complicated.

The new economic difficulties which regimes faced were compounded by political failures in less developed countries during the age of hubris. Socioeconomic reforms—land reforms, for example—had often failed to materialize, because powerful vested interests had persuaded politicians not to pursue them vigorously, and/or because those leaders had underestimated the difficulty of implementing the reforms. When these things happened, ordinary people compared their current experiences not with the colonial era but with the more recent past, when hopes had still been high and patronage systems had worked at least a little more effectively. This triggered a loss of confidence in leaders, regimes and patronage systems which—while they entailed some decentralization of resources—were still quite centralized in character.

It took time for people and politicians in less developed countries to recognize the limits of charismatic leadership and of corporatism—both of which implied commandism—whether or not they were reinforced by patronage systems. But in the 1970s, especially after the oil shocks of 1973–74 and 1978–79, their inadequacies became vividly apparent almost everywhere. Autocratic regimes, which were especially dependent on economic performance to sustain their legitimacy, faced particularly severe difficulties—usually including inflation, soaring debt burdens, and little or no economic growth (Huntington, 1992).

Their problems were compounded by the tendency of nearly all regimes in the postwar era, including patent autocracies, "to accept—if not to implement—the rhetoric and ideas of democracy...Explicit argument against democracy as a concept almost disappeared from public debate in most countries of the world. 'For the first time in the history of the world,' a UNESCO report noted in 1951, 'no doctrines are advanced as anti-democratic' (Huntington, 1992, p. 47).

This eventually helped to persuade a number of nondemocratic regimes to undertake democratic decentralization. And yet most politicians in such regimes initially reacted to these problems of centralism not by decentralizing, but by doing the opposite.

Their responses varied somewhat. Military and bureaucratic authoritarianism across much of Latin America became more, not less commandist during the 1970s (O'Donnell, 1973). Indeed, "centralized, top-down approaches dominated governance" across a diversity of Latin American countries well into the 1980s (Fox, 1994, p. 105). One-party systems in most of Africa relied increasingly on coercion to maintain their control. Leaders as different as Mao Zedong, Indira Gandhi, Ferdinand Marcos and Daniel Arap Moi set about deinstitutionalizing in the interests of personal dominance. This implied still greater, if less effective and therefore more alienating, centralization.[6] But despite variations, the general tendency towards centralizing responses to a crisis of the centralized state was apparent and tended to make things worse, not better.

Leaders in less developed countries, and especially in the development agencies that provided them with advisors, retained much of their confidence in techniques for gathering and interpreting quantitative data—a task which nearly always rested with central governments and enhanced their assertiveness. This was in one way surprising, since the problems which Robert McNamara had encountered very publicly over Vietnam indicated that in less developed countries such techniques could be—to put it mildly—unreliable. But the refinement of these techniques and the rapid development of hardware to facilitate them, encouraged regimes to persist in the belief that they were better informed than ever before, and that they need not listen to or yield decisionmaking power to local communities.

Notes

1. I am grateful to Keith Bezanson for reminding me of this.
2. I am grateful to Geoffrey Hawthorn for stressing this.
3. I am grateful to V.K. Natraj of the University of Mysore for sharing his work in progress on these issues with me.
4. Kasfir here cites Wraith, 1972, p. 218 and Mulasa, 1970, p. 250.
5. I am grateful to Keith Bezanson for help on this point.
6. This trend was widespread, but not universal. For example in Cuba emphasis shifted from charismatic leadership to a more routinized approach, using the party to impose more systematic control—although this also yielded greater centralization (Dominguez, 1986). Huntington reminds us that a few of these regimes also resorted to military adventures which failed, further undermining their legitimacy (Huntington, 1992, pp. 54–56).

Part III
Explaining the Latest Wave of
Decentralizations

Why have so many governments across the world undertaken one or another type of decentralization since the early 1980s? To explain this, we need to consider both grand themes and more modest trends. The first section, below, assesses what appear to be changes in basic conditions, and in the temper of the times—and dismisses a few things which had little impact. The second section briefly links these with decentralizing politicians' mixed motives and objectives. The third section considers a body of work which advances, within limits, our understanding both of the origins and of the implications of decentralization. That will open the way to a more detailed discussion of the promise and limitations of decentralization in the last three parts of this study. The discussion here is intended as a corrective to the exceedingly brief, incomplete and unsatisfactory explanation provided in the *World Development Report 1997* (World Bank, 1997a).

It is important to stress that no single cause, or even a small number of them, triggered decisions to decentralize. These were, ultimately, *political* decisions, and as Huntington has reminded us, "In politics, almost everything has many causes....To occur historically, an event almost has to be overdetermined theoretically" (Huntington, 1992, p. 37). This certainly applies here—especially, as we shall see, because many analysts tend to believe that underlying material conditions (mainly fiscal crises) came close to determining decisions to decentralize.

To clarify this, it is worth paraphrasing Huntington (1992, p. 38), who was discussing democratization. The causes of decentralization differ substantially from one place to another. The multiplicity of theories and the diversity of experiences suggest the probable validity of the following propositions:

- No single factor is sufficient to explain decisions to decentralize in all countries or in a single country.
- No single factor is necessary to decisions to decentralize in all countries.
- Decentralization in each country is the result of a combination of causes.

- The combination of causes producing decentralization varies from country to country.[1]

We can add a further point which we made at the start of this paper—decentralization has been attempted by an great diversity of regimes: the solvent and the insolvent, autocracies and democracies, and governments of the left, right and center. This also suggests that a diversity of influences has been at work, and that decentralization has been undertaken for a variety of motives and with a variety of goals in mind.

Here, as in Part II above, we need to focus mainly on how politicians think and react to the trends and problems which confront them. They are usually assisted by technocrats with expertise in the social sciences, but it is political leaders who nearly always make the key decisions about decentralization. Since politicians tend to be short of time and tranquility in which to weigh policy decisions, and preoccupied with short-term trends and current problems, the impact of deeper causes is usually filtered through the distorting lens of these more immediate considerations.[2]

In the section just below we (again inevitably) offer social scientists less rigor than they might like. And since we are dealing with even more recent events than in Part II, historians will have even more reasons to feel uneasy. To make matters worse, there is a shortage of evidence on why and how decisions were made to decentralize. But let us nevertheless see whether what emerges is persuasive.

Diverse Causes

We began to explore some of these things in the discussion of centralized, commandist approaches to governance in "The Unraveling" in Part II above. The degeneration of patronage systems and ruling parties in less developed countries played a role. The regimes faced mounting demands from organized interests, yet sluggish economic growth and increasing corruption by political activists at all levels undermined their ability to respond to those demands. The oil shocks of the mid- and late-1970s compounded that problem and caused others. Many national leaders overcentralized power in the interests of personal rule, and that undermined the autonomy, resources, effectiveness and responsiveness of ruling parties and formal institutions. Ordinary folk grew impatient with the failure of governments to deliver not only prosperity but social reform. This eroded their belief in the charismatic qualities, and even the benign intentions, of national leaders.

There were other things at work too. By the late 1970s, it was becoming increasingly possible for small enterprises in many sectors to compete with larger companies—including state-owned enterprises. This was partly the result of technological innovations, but their main advantages (sometimes aided by technology) were their flexibility and their capacity to react quickly to changing conditions and consumer appetites (see for example, Piore and Sabel, 1984). This impelled all manner of decisionmakers towards greater decentralization. These things were occurring mostly in industrialized nations, but they were (at least imperfectly) perceived in many less developed countries as well. The temper of the times was changing, and decentralization was in the air.

Like Keynesian and Leninist approaches to economies, the two paradigms which had long dominated political analyses of less developed countries—the political development/modernization school and dependency theory—became increasingly less convincing during the 1980s. New modes of analysis gained popularity in their place and helped to prepare the ground for experiments with decentralization (Manor, 1991). Three are worth mentioning (Blair, 1995).

Analysts employing public choice approaches began to see democratic decentralization as an option which offers something resembling a free market—bringing together "buyers" (citizens) and "sellers" (decentralized authorities) in a setting where the wishes of the former can impinge effectively on the latter (Smith, 1985). Specialists in public finance and advocates of the new institutional economics—who, together with the public choice school, pursue institutional analysis approaches to public policy—developed arguments which also lent momentum to the fashion for decentralization, especially of the democratic type.

These analysts saw democratic decentralization as a means of linking political demand for services with a requirement that beneficiaries pay for them. Our evidence suggests that this actually occurs much less often than analysts might have wished, but the appeal of this idea clearly strengthened the initial case for decentralization. They were also attracted by the opportunity which democratic decentralization appeared to offer to off-load obligations from hard-pressed central governments onto local- and intermediate-level bodies, and to facilitate cuts in public expenditure. Our evidence again shows that democratic decentralization often ends up increasing overall government expenditures—especially, but not only, in the early stages—and that when expenditures are not increased, and tasks are simply off-loaded in the hope that local resources will fund them, this can result in system failure.[3] But once again, this idea fueled enthusiasm for decentralization (Blair, 1995).

These new modes of analysis gained ground at the same time as Western donor agencies sought increasingly to promote good governance in developing countries. Their agendas contained diverse and perhaps mutually contradictory elements, but by the early 1980s, some of these agencies were beginning to press regimes in the South to democratize and (much less often) to decentralize.

During the 1980s, some donor agencies also began to shift their emphases away from large-scale development programs to more modest, microlevel projects into which grass roots communities could be drawn as participants, in the hope of making development more sustainable. This owed something to the psychological residue from the American defeat in Vietnam which eroded confidence in the efficacy of giant, massive state undertakings. More important perhaps was the growing suspicion that integrated rural development programs had serious shortcomings. These had been one last predominantly top-down attempt to respond to the disillusionment with centralized governance. The problems that they encountered caused many politicians in less developed countries to wonder whether any initiative from the apex of political systems could work. These changes of perception helped open the way to decentralization.

It must be stressed, however, that decisions to decentralize were seldom donor-driven. The World Bank and the International Monetary Fund tended to lag behind governments in less developed countries. They were alerted to the promise of decentralization mainly by changes that occurred in Latin America—especially in Chile and Brazil.[4] But serious reservations remain (to this day) in both institutions about the dangers which it poses, especially to macroeconomic management (see for example, Prud'homme, 1995; and Tanzi, 1996).

The influence of World Bank representatives on government thinking about decentralization in East Africa—which appears to be fairly typical—has been ambiguous, but on balance negative even in quite recent times. On the one hand, pressure on governments to undertake civil service reform has lately helped to persuade the Tanzanian Prime Minister to transfer implementation powers from central ministries to the private sector, new executive agencies and (very recently) to elected local authorities. On the other hand, World Bank representatives in Tanzania and Uganda have focused their attention in civil service reform on central ministries, without seeking to link it to decentralization. This has delayed decisions by those governments to couple such reform to advances in decentralization—decisions which were taken by politicians in those countries despite World Bank advice.[5]

Some bilateral agencies were quicker to recognize the promise of decentralization, but they tended to support decentralized institutions *once they were created* rather than pressuring recipient governments to experiment anew with decentralization.[6] *In seeking explanations for the popularity of decentralization, we must therefore look mainly at the thinking of leaders within the governments of developing countries.*

The democratization of numerous formerly autocratic regimes—especially, but not only in Latin America during the 1980s (and again in Eastern Europe since 1989)—"exposed a gulf between the state and civil society that could no longer be attributed" to autocratic rule. This led to greater interest in

> greater political accountability...And local government, because of its proximity to civil society, was seen as a crucial mechanism for...bridging the gap between the state and civil society, and in transforming hitherto marginalized groups into full-fledged citizens (Nickson, 1995, p. 2).

The collapse of the Soviet system and the end of the Cold War have also played a role here. While that war lasted, governments on both sides felt pressure to maintain commandist postures in order to pursue the struggle effectively. Thereafter it was easier to relax and devolve power and resources. But we should not exaggerate here. Note, crucially, that interest in decentralization had crystallized in a great many countries well *before* Communist regimes broke down and the Cold War ceased. The main effect of those events was to intensify interest in decentralization which was already present.

The disintegration of the USSR further eroded the already substantially discredited notion that commandism could be effective and popular. And because it undermined belief in undemocratic approaches to governance, it helped to open the way to decentralization of the democratic variety. It eased the anxieties of rightist and center-right regimes in many developing countries about the Communist threat—anxieties which had encouraged centralization. It also eased similar American anxieties which had inspired efforts to prop up rightist autocracies.

Indeed, Nickson (1995) has noted that many regimes in Latin America had defined the "democracy" which they claimed to be defending with reference to foreign rather than domestic considerations. Right-of-center governments had pursued commandist, often downright autocratic approaches in the name of defending democracy from international Communism. Leftist governments, who were worried about threats from American anti-Communists, had behaved similarly—again on grounds that they were protecting democracy. The end of the Cold War removed much of the justification for either of these things. It refocused attention on domestic politics, and when that happened the shortcomings of commandism were more starkly exposed. These trends in Latin America were paralleled to some extent in parts of East and Southeast Asia—again in ways that made decentralization seem more promising and feasible.

Has pressure from ordinary people at the grass roots persuaded central authorities in some countries to decentralize? The answer must be: hardly at all. There is some evidence from a small number of countries—in India, Tanzania, Brazil and Colombia, for example—of elites at intermediate levels having an impact[7] or, in South Korea, of opposition parties lobbying effectively for devolution.[8] However, the channels through which such demands can be transmitted upward through the political system are often so poorly developed that little headway can be made. But in any case, widespread, popular pressure from the local level is something else, and it was largely absent in these and other cases.

Some scholars *presume* that such sentiments exist at the local level, as do some political parties. See, for example, one study of Thailand (Medhi, 1995). Perhaps there is clear evidence of those sentiments, but none is presented in that paper, and there is next to none available from any other country. Until we see such evidence, we must attach the Scottish verdict "not proven" to claims that mass enthusiasm for decentralization either existed prior to decentralization or has had an impact on policymakers. Enthusiasm often develops after decentralization takes place, but that is a different thing.

What we do see, in Thailand and some countries which (unlike it) have experienced some significant decentralization to the local level, is an interest among elite political activists at or near that level for decentralization. But their sentiments have had much less impact than the (often accurate) insight among high-level politicians and technocrats in a modest number of countries that decentralization would be seized upon avidly by local communities—who had voiced no demand for it—and put to creative use.

The architect of devolution in the Indian state of Karnataka[9] understood this, as have policymakers in, for example, Namibia and South Africa. World Bank officials working on northeast Brazil may also have shared these views. But they appear at this writing to be rather rare exceptions. Even when this recognition has played a part, it is not the same thing as local communities, or nongovernmental organizations working among them, pressing for it.

To say this is not to deny that a social and political awakening has been occurring in a great many developing countries over the last two decades.[10] Voluntary associations and indigenous nongovernmental organizations have blossomed impressively in many countries (although this has been exaggerated by some enthusiasts for it). Civil society more broadly has developed and begun to assert itself across much of the South—not least because of frustration with centralized modes of governance. These changes owe something to the fiscal problems of national governments, but as the preceding (and, indeed, the following) discussion indicates, that was only one of many elements in the story.

The decline of the old popular belief in the heroic qualities of central political leaders—which makes senior figures in the private sector seem relatively more trustworthy, and helps to open up systems to market forces—has also inclined many people to place greater faith in leaders at intermediate and local levels. But the effect of this political awakening was not to create mass pressure from the grass roots for decentralization, but rather to persuade leaders atop political systems to consider decentralization, in order to cope more effectively with emerging social forces.

At the risk of stressing the obvious, let us consider this in a little more detail. Many political leaders have found it harder than before to make the machinery of government engage effectively with society—especially with those social groups which are politically aware and which are or wish to be politically active. This has happened in many places because the structures which once knit state and society together (after a fashion) have decayed. These structures include the formal institutions of state and informal institutions, such as political parties' organizations, patronage systems, and others.

But even where these structures have not decayed, changes in society often mean that if the old structures merely stand still, they become less able than before to engage with society. This is where the social and political awakening comes in. It has made at least some (and often most) social groups more aware, assertive and impatient. This generates both an overload of demands upon governments and increased conflict—either between social groups and governments, or between social groups, or both.

This is often attended by an influx of people into politics, at least onto the margins of the political system, as new sociopolitical movements develop beyond the reach of the preexisting government and party machinery. These people often have unrealistic expectations of politics and they are always difficult for the old structures to manage. Old slogans, promises, enticements, threats and references to danger posed by nefarious forces (internal or external) fail to enable government to cope with social forces.

This sort of thing can happen for a diversity of reasons. Political management becomes more difficult if a regime introduces major changes in policy (structural adjustment packages, for example) which place certain interests under severe strain, or which alter the basis of its legitimacy. The latter has happened, for example, in China since 1978 (Saich, 1993). If rapid economic growth creates severe inequalities, or if it damages the environment in ways that deprive large groups of their means of livelihood, it can create dangerous alienation among those who lose out. This is apparent, for example, in parts of Southeast Asia.[11]

People who *benefit* from rapid growth can also pose problems for politicians, often at the same time as governments face difficulties from losers. Much of this will be familiar to readers. The middle classes, especially those who derive great self-esteem from increasing wealth and precious skills, aspire to a greater political say. So do prosperous rural dwellers who may not qualify, strictly speaking, as middle class. Workers whose wages rise as growth proceeds seek political rights and more even-handed treatment by the government in their dealings with employers.

In countries where economic growth is sluggish, similar problems arise. The resources which governments distribute among social groups to gain their support or acquiescence fail to expand quickly enough to keep pace with population growth or rising political demands. This has happened in oil-producing rentier states when petroleum prices fall, and in countries whose economies depend on other raw materials or crops.[12] It has also occurred in places like India, where ruling parties have sustained themselves through the politics of resource distribution.

We see here that both economic success and economic failure can generate pressure for political change. It is thus not surprising that decentralization has been attempted both in newly prosperous countries and in those facing severe resource constraints. Politicians in both situations, and in more ambiguous circumstances, have seen decentralization as a way to reconnect their regimes with social groups, to sustain or revive their party organizations, and to provide opportunities for people at local and intermediate levels who want a political voice.

Once a few leaders began experimenting with decentralization, the great advances in communications that had occurred by the 1980s and 1990s made it more likely that others would learn about and seek to replicate their efforts. This has also facilitated the spread of democratization at the national level. Improved communications make it easier for politicians to see not only that leaders in other countries were decentralizing, but how they are going about it (Huntington, 1992, p. 101).

They usually learned of these changes so early—thanks to improved communications—that what they were seeing was that leaders elsewhere were decentralizing in response to problems similar to their own—but not that decentralization was solving those problems. Too little time had elapsed for them to conclude that. In other words, decisions to decentralize were made not because its utility had been proven, but because it appeared possible that it could help them to cope with the loss of popular confidence in the centralized state. This is an important distinction, to which we shall return.

It is important that we note four further things which largely or entirely fail to qualify as causes of the recent wave of decentralizations. We have already discussed the first of these. Since decentralization has been undertaken both by regimes which had succeeded and by regimes which had failed economically (and indeed, by governments with ambiguous records), there is reason to suspect that no set of economic conditions has been a particularly important cause of decisions to decentralize. (This theme arises again, later, when we consider the type of analysis that Charles Tilly and others have developed.)

Second, the challenges of globalization have not had much impact. This is true partly because they have only become fully apparent to governments in quite recent years, *after* most decisions to decentralize were taken. But more importantly, governments which fear that they are losing control of things like international trade, telecommunications and the like, over which they once exercised great influence, are liable to become less, not more likely to devolve further powers onto lower level authorities. So it is arguable that decentralization has occurred despite, not because of, globalization.

Third, the recent surge in ethnic conflicts around the world does not appear to have done much to encourage decentralization. In theory, a country which suffers from tensions between ethnic groups that tend to inhabit different regions might ease this problem by providing regions with a degree of autonomy. But there is precious little evidence that this has actually happened in recent years. Such an attempt was initiated in Sri Lanka in 1995, but at this writing there are grave doubts about whether it will make much headway. Such considerations had an influence in South Africa, but the main concern there was the deepening of democracy. Another possible example comes from Nigeria, but in a much earlier period. The number of states in that federal system was increased in 1976, after the Biafra war, to fragment the regions within which different ethnic groups resided—although little actual devolution took place.[13] But in the absence of much further recent evidence, there seems little reason to see ethnic tension as an important spur to decentralization.

Fourth, neither extensive previous experience with decentralization nor the lack thereof appears to have inclined regimes to decentralize in recent times. The list of developing countries with such experience includes the Philippines, most of Commonwealth South Asia and Commonwealth Africa.

Decentralization has until recent years been largely untried in francophone and lusophone Africa,[14] the Middle East, Latin America,[15] and most of East and Southeast Asia. Many former Communist countries in Europe and Asia had what might appear to be local- or intermediate-level authorities. But since in practice these institutions tended to project the influence of the central party or state into lower level arenas, they cannot be regarded as precedents for what has happened more recently in some of these countries.

If we consider what actually happened in several of the countries with extensive previous experience, we discover considerable diversity. Elected officials were given extensive powers at lower levels of the system in the Philippines in 1901, soon after the Americans assumed control there. But since this occurred before bureaucratic agencies at those levels had acquired substance, elected officials tended to fill bureaucratic posts with cronies. This severely undermined the effectiveness, responsiveness and probity of local authorities there.[16]

Sri Lanka had local councils which were elected and were overseen by an elected minister from 1931 onwards. But two things prevented them from acquiring the powers and resources to perform well—suspicions among other ministers that the empowerment of these bodies would give too much influence to the Minister of Local Administration, and the belief among leaders from the Sinhalese majority that generosity towards such councils would be seen as a concession to the Tamil minority (Manor, 1989). That latter consideration has crippled decentralized institutions there until very recently (Manor, 1979).

The influence of Gandhian ideas in India has always ensured a somewhat wider constituency for decentralization than in most other countries. But the lack of enthusiasm for such views in Nehru's circle and among India's constitution-makers (Nehru, 1960, and Austin, 1966) ensured that the elected councils which were created during the 1950s at local and intermediate levels had only very limited powers. Thereafter, national leaders' preoccupations with large-scale development projects and state-level politicians' aversion to sharing power with elected members of lower level councils largely thwarted decentralization (Mehta, 1978).

Bangladesh has long had elected councils standing just above the local level, although at most times these have lacked the resources to accomplish anything significant. Prior to the mid-1980s, it saw two military dictators (one as part of Pakistan, and one after its creation in 1971) develop more extensive and somewhat better funded systems of decentralized institutions. But neither of those experiments yielded many tangible development benefits, and both were tainted by their association with rulers who were essentially autocratic centralizers.

In the 1950s, the British created elected local bodies with limited powers in their African colonies. After the colonies achieved independence, the general pattern (with some variations) was for these institutions to be turned into de facto extensions of the ruling parties which governed in a highly centralized manner, then to be allowed to decay, and finally to be abolished or to fall into utter disuse. The record of decentralization in Commonwealth Africa before the mid-1980s is thus largely one of failure. The experiences of these nations have been sufficiently uninspiring and variegated that we cannot say shared happy memories has caused the recent wave of decentralizations.

In other countries, with little or no previous history of decentralization, has the very lack of experience somehow inclined them to attempt this in recent years? Again, the answer must be no—partly because it is nearly impossible to prove a negative, but mainly because there is next to no evidence to support this notion.

Given all of this, we are driven back to the conclusion that the main explanation for the inclination among politicians to decentralize must lie in the widespread but rather vague sense in many nations that centralized structures had fallen well short of adequacy. This shortfall was evident in poor economic performance, but in politicians' minds, that was only one of the dimensions of the problem—and not the most important one. They tended strongly to conceive of their predicament mainly in political terms. Rightly or wrongly, that is the way they think.

And, to reiterate, few (if any) decentralizers since the early 1980s have acted on solid evidence of its utility. We will see in Part IV of this study evidence of the promise of democratic decentralization for rural development, but almost all of this information was unavailable to the politicians who have recently decided to decentralize.

Mixed Motives

Recall the vague nature of the widespread notion that centralized governance had failed. This vagueness made it possible for the idea of decentralization to appeal to a wide diversity of regimes facing a variety of problems. It also made decentralization attractive to politicians with diverse motives. And because the unease with commandism was so vague, it offered few clear and specific signposts to help leaders choose particular forms of decentralization. As a result, the processes which then developed in various countries varied from place to place.

Recall also that would be decentralizers had little or no empirical evidence to indicate what decentralization could and could not achieve, or how specific types of decentralization would produce specific results. This again left their options wide open. They were therefore free to act on a variety of motives. We need to consider these, to understand how varied their calculations, and the reforms which they undertook were.

Most decentralizers have operated with mixed motives and objectives. They have often proceeded on the basis both of statesmanlike considerations, seeking the genuine empowerment of groups at lower levels, and of hard-nosed calculations of self-interest. In the discussion that follows, we separate these kinds of calculations rather artificially, treating them as ideal types.

Elements of these ideal types tend to get bound up with one another. It is not just that individual politicians have mixed motives. Governments are not monolithic: different actors within them perceive policies differently. This has tended to produce experiments with decentralization which are curious, incongruous hybrids—which do not necessarily give way to neat syntheses, but which persist far longer than we might expect (Chai-Anan, 1991). This naturally makes the outcomes of these experiments rather ambiguous. The ambiguities are addressed in Parts IV and VI of this study. Let us consider these ideal types.

Genuine attempts at empowerment. The list of cases that bear some resemblance to this ideal type includes South Africa, Namibia, some Indian states (notably West Bengal and Karnataka in the 1980s), the Philippines, Bolivia and others. They have tended to proceed with many of the following purposes in mind:

- Deepen democracy by extending liberal representative politics to lower levels
- Enlarge opportunities for citizens to participate in decisions affecting their lives
- Draw on local knowledge and preferences about development
- Bring informal local mechanisms for the management of resources or the resolution of conflicts into the formal political process
- Promote partnership between state and society
- Give interests at lower levels a greater sense of ownership of development projects, thus making projects more sustainable
- Enhance associational activity at lower levels
- Facilitate cooperation between government and lower level associations and nongovernmental organizations
- Enhance the accountability of bureaucrats, elected representatives

and political institutions more generally
- Enhance the responsiveness of government
- Enhance the transparency of government
- Ease the frustrations of people with political ambitions at lower levels by enabling them to play official roles
- Equip people with skills at representation, bargaining, and so forth, which develop in democratic systems and which make those systems more sustainable
- Improve the collective action potential of rural dwellers, and acquaint them with "lobbying technology" (Becker, 1985)
- Promote monitoring, evaluation and planning from below
- Undermine "authoritarian enclaves" (if they exist) by creating democratic institutions in subregions or localities where autocratic forces held sway
- Ease the alienation of opposition parties and social groups that lack influence in the central government, by giving them opportunities to hold power in lower level arenas (a consideration in, for example, the new South Africa)[17]
- Promote a more equitable distribution of resources, either by giving remote, poor and previously underrepresented areas greater resources and influence, or by uniting prosperous areas with nearby, poorer, areas, under single lower level authorities (again, as in the new South Africa or Namibia (Simon, 1993)
- Alleviate poverty
- Empower women
- Create a counterweight to urban bias by giving rural areas greater representation, autonomy and resources
- Enhance the legitimacy of the political system.

Even when governments decentralize with most of these worthy objectives in mind, plenty of things can go wrong, and the fulfillment of some of them can produce ironic or unhappy results, as we will see in Parts IV and VI of this study. But despite this, experiments which grow out of such thinking stand a good chance of achieving considerable success.

Decentralization for narrow or partisan advantage. Some of the items in the list below are the product of cynicism, but many are not. Not all of the items below present outright contradictions to those in the list above. But there are often serious dissonances between these and the items set out above.

- Democratize lower levels in the political system as a substitute for democratization at the apex

- Draw powerful figures at local levels into official positions of power, so that the central government can cultivate them as allies
- Off-load tasks which the central government finds costly or inconvenient, or both, onto lower level authorities
- Mobilize local resources through tax increases, the blame for which will be borne by people at lower levels
- Obtain local resources which the ruling party can exploit for partisan advantage (as in Ghana—see Crook and Manor, 1994)
- Get voters in elections to lower level authorities to do central leaders' dirty work, by ridding the ruling party of undesirable politicians at lower levels (as in Côte d'Ivoire—see Faure, 1989)
- Give the appearance of democratizing lower levels in the system, while actually limiting the influence of elected members of authorities to such an extent that what mainly occurs is deconcentration— the dispersal of central administrators into lower level arenas—which strengthens the central government's power
- Distract their countrymen and outside observers from other coercive actions of the central government[18]
- Please donor agencies who favor decentralization
- Assist the ruling party in building its organization by providing seats on lower level authorities, to which party members can be elected.

We will see in Parts IV and VI below that the incongruous mixtures of these two types of motives can produce unexpected results. Even when a government adopts policies mainly for reasons set out in the first list above, surprising things can happen—not least because the empowerment of lower levels brings new groups with their own priorities into the political game. And governments with more self-interested or even cynical motives sometimes find that decentralized institutions take on a life of their own, with unanticipated consequences.

But the purpose of setting out these different sets of motives and objectives here is to indicate that the explanation for the recent wave of decentralizations is complex, and that political considerations—which predominate in the lists above—tend to loom large. It is important to bear this in mind as we consider, in the next section, another set of explanations for policy innovations.

Linking the Origins, Institutionalization, and Implications of Decentralization

To enhance our understanding of the material presented above on the decline of confidence in centralized approaches to governance and the growing inclination in recent years to decentralize, let us now turn to a body of work that seeks to explain other major changes. It deals both with the origins and the implications of change. This impels us to consider both with regard to decentralization.

This analysis pays special attention to the work of the historian Charles Tilly on the rise and evolution of European states since the tenth century. But it also considers the work of a number of other scholars, many of them economists, on the origins of various types of policy change in quite recent times. These are usefully surveyed in a World Bank study (Binswanger and Deininger, 1997).

This discussion does not seek to replicate Tilly's analysis. In several important respects, his concerns differ from ours. For him, the main issue is how "extraction and struggle over the means of war created the central organizational structures of states" (Tilly, 1992, p. 15). We saw in Part II that the waging of the World War II had an enormous impact on state structures, both in the industrialized nations and in their colonies. But our focus is on the postwar era.

The decentralizing assessed here was the result not of the need to prepare for war, but of its absence and of the inappropriate approaches to governance which wartime conditions bequeathed to later generations. Tilly is naturally preoccupied with the coercive doings of governments that attend war-making, while we focus on one of the ways in which governments have sought to develop noncoercive means of relating to their societies.

Tilly concentrates, much of the time, on interstate relations, while this study deals mainly with intrastate issues. Finally, he carefully notes that his analysis is particular to Europe, and that the "non-European experience will be different" (Tilly, 1992, p. 16).

Nevertheless, several elements of Tilly's inquiry are helpful here. We will see repeatedly that studies by Tilly and other scholars reviewed by Binswanger and Deininger—up to a point—in enriching our understanding of the origins, institutionalization and implications of decentralization. But they also have their limitations, for three main reasons. They sometimes examine other eras and parts of the world. They deal with other types of policy innovations. And they overemphasize both the calculations of technocrats (when it is politicians who make the final decisions) and, especially, the importance of material conditions in shaping policy decisions. The empirical evidence on decentralization indicates that such conditions rarely determined such decisions, and that decentralizers were often more preoccupied with the political considerations discussed in the preceding sections of this study.

The politicians who ultimately chose to decentralize considered a wider set of issues than the literature under review can accommodate.

They had a less tidy understanding of the problems and options which faced them than their technocratic advisors did and than that literature suggests. And when they got down to the business of policy innovation, they were often so short of time and so preoccupied with short-term problems that they undertook confused, ambiguous actions.

With this in mind, let us consider the utility and limitations of the literature under review. Tilly calls our attention to "capital-intensive societies." In contrast to "coercive societies," they developed representative institutions through a process of bargaining in which interest groups on whom states were substantially dependent for revenues compelled rulers to provide mechanisms through which their views could be represented.

There are clear echoes here with the process that led to decentralization. One recent study (Moore, 1997) points to a correlation between the dependence of governments on tax revenues from interests within their countries and a tendency to undertake "good governance" reforms. That insight is useful in an investigation of where decentralization has and has not occurred. It is not surprising, for example, that the list of countries where decentralization has *not* occurred includes most of the rentier states that mainly derive their revenues from oil exports.

There are, however, limits to the utility of this explanation. Many regimes which depend heavily on taxes paid by their domestic populations have declined to decentralize, or have pretended fraudulently to have done so—mainly for their own political reasons. Some (though not all) of the African countries and Asian newly industrializing countries fall into this category. On the other hand, some governments which are substantially dependent on foreign aid decentralized, even before aid donors began pressing for such reforms (Bangladesh under Ershad in 1985 is an example)—again, for their own political reasons.

Another important insight from the literature under review applies to two critical concerns here—the origins of recent decentralizations and their institutionalization. This is the idea that attempts at policy reform

> are most likely to be initiated and succeed when the state is facing fiscal crisis, and...efficiency-enhancing policies will be sustained only when groups that benefit from the policies defend them against pressure from groups that benefit from the alternatives (Binswanger and Deininger, 1997, p. 38).

This is helpful, within limits, in explaining the origins of recent experiments with decentralization. The economic shocks of the 1970s and the resulting resource constraints faced by governments often contributed to the perceptions which led to decentralization. But because the shocks were less severe than those on which the literature fixes (deep economic depressions, the Black Death, and the like), very few regimes felt compelled to decentralize as a direct result of the crises. The contribution of the shocks tended to be less potent and more indirect, in that they dented politicians' confidence in the capacities of central governments and in commandist modes of governance. Note also that the list of decentralizing governments contains many which did not face particularly serious resource constraints, as well as many that did.

Still fewer regimes decentralized as a result of two themes stressed by Marxist writers whose work formed part of the literature under review. They argue that political reforms occur because the dominant classes see them it as a way to further their economic interests, or because alignments of class forces compel leaders to seek allies among less prosperous groups who might benefit.

It is difficult to find evidence of decentralizers reckoning that their reforms would assist—or, in many cases, have the least thing to do with—the economic interests of powerful groups. They almost always saw it (rightly or wrongly) as predominantly a political change, which would not greatly affect the economic sphere. When they thought in terms of other spheres of life in which decentralization might have an impact, most of them tended to think first of society (improvements in state-society relations) and sometimes culture (making government more sensitive to religious and ethnic minorities, and to local knowledge and cultural particularities), rather than of economics. The same cannot, of course, be said of economic reforms, but it is broadly true of decisions to decentralize.

When policymakers considered where gains and losses might occur through decentralization, they thought about levels in the political system, not class or other social forces. Decentralization has occurred amid such a great diversity of class alignments that there seems little connection between them and it. These arguments are of little help to us here.

Nor does the recent wave of decentralizations provide examples of "asset-owning elites" at lower levels "imposing their will...and compromising the power of public institutions" or forcing institutional change. The recent international enthusiasm for decentralization differs in that respect from the process of European state formation. We are not witnessing "subnational fractions...(coming) to dominate national policy making" (Bates and Lien, 1985, drawing on North, 1981, and Levi, 1981). Almost none of these experiments with decentralization originated from power struggles between forces at higher and lower levels. Most decentralizers have conceived and implemented these reforms from above, on their own initiative, relatively free of pressure from below, mainly to enhance the state's capacity for noncoercive governance.

This raises doubts about what some of this literature has to say about the nature of the state. Most decentralizing governments under study here are not acting like "predatory revenue maximizers" (Bates and Lien, 1985, p. 55). Instead, they are behaving like canny political bargainers extending their bases through accommodation. When a great many governments all over the world put care and effort into decentralization—even though they think that it will have little impact on revenues—it strongly suggests that states amount to much more than mere "predatory revenue maximizers." Their motives are more complex than those words imply, and political considerations tend to take precedence over revenue concerns.

Decentralizing governments have also tended to grasp that partnerships with groups at lower levels would make development more sustainable. Consider, for example, the new bargains that decentralized authorities often facilitate between central governments and important social groups at lower levels. Their principal utility is not as a means of persuading interest groups to provide revenues to the state, but as a way of cultivating political support and of enhancing regime legitimacy.

We need to deal carefully with this point. We see in Part VI that decentralization has—*thus far*, in a process which has only recently begun—had very little impact on states' ability to mobilize resources from their populations to meet the cost of public goods. This is likely to change, at least somewhat, for the better over the medium and longer term. As decentralization improves government responsiveness, draws society into creative partnerships with the state's decentralized institutions, makes many different types of policies more sustainable, and erodes the suspicion and even cynicism which ordinary folk often feel towards government—as these things occur, additional resource mobilization ought to become more likely. But it is impossible to predict with confidence how much more of this may become possible, or how quickly it will happen. It has clearly not happened yet, and few politicians who have decentralized expect it to happen soon. So to reiterate, decentralizers have tended to act mainly for *political* reasons, some of which are far less momentous than the causal forces assessed in the literature under discussion here.

Some of the calculations by politicians which lay behind decisions to decentralize were related to the predominantly materialist themes that emerge from this literature. But most were connected to them rather tenuously or not at all. The closest link can be found in the perception among many politicians who depended heavily on patronage distribution, that resource constraints threatened this type of politics (see Binswanger and Deininger, 1997). Corruption and demand overload had undermined patronage systems, even before the oil shocks of the 1970s, and the stringencies that followed made things far worse.

In the teeth of this problem, political leaders *might* have viewed decentralization as a means of providing people at the grass roots with a new kind of politics which would divert their attention and their demands away from the increasingly ineffective networks of patronage distribution, and toward authorities at intermediate and local levels, and new opportunities to influence decisions at those levels.

Politicians seldom developed this view, however. Many saw decentralization not as an alternative to patronage systems, but as a device to extend and renew those systems. Most of those politicians also had too little time, tranquility and sophistication to perceive fully that a new kind of politics was being created. They only half-sensed it, vaguely amid an array of other sometimes petty concerns that dominated their daily routines. One exception was P.V. Narasimha Rao, who pushed through constitutional amendments requiring decentralization in every Indian state. He articulated an impressive understanding of this (in private).[19] But among decentralizers, he was highly unusual.

Fiscal problems inspired one further thought in decentralizers' minds which might appear trivial to the scholars—mainly economists—whom Binswanger and Deininger survey, but which weighed mightily with many politicians. Resource constraints were making politics boring.

It was boring for the politicians whose lives now consisted of modest adjustments to distinctly unambitious policies—which usually entailed decisions not to create but to reduce or eliminate. Still worse, from the politicians' point of view, the politicians themselves were becoming boring to ordinary folk. The excitement of the old pioneering days had gone out of politics. That was in some ways quite useful for political stability, since it scaled down expectations to realistic levels, but it deprived politicians of much of their former appeal. This problem afflicts regimes not just in developing countries, but everywhere—in, for example, France. The politics of modest adjustments is not the politics of grandeur (Domenach, 1997; Hoffman, 1997).

Given all of this, the fiscal straitening of the 1980s and 1990s impelled politicians to search for initiatives that would be inexpensive, but at least modestly exciting and pioneering. Decentralization clearly qualifies. It has been advertised in slogans like Rajiv Gandhi's in the late 1980s: "We have given you power."[20]

Note, however, that decentralization also creates conditions in which national leaders will never be quite so exciting again—because it means that they have abandoned much of their former power to set agendas and determine the allocation of public resources. That does not mean that decentralization weakens them. It is more accurate to say that it requires them to trade one sort of power for another. It weakens the state in some ways, while strengthening it in others which are potentially more advantageous to national leaders. They are trading the power to command and excite for the opportunity to be more responsive and, thereby, perhaps to survive longer in power. (We will return to this presently, when we examine the ways in which decentralization strengthens the state.)

Other considerations, which relate more tenuously to the themes that emerge from this literature, carried great weight with politicians. Many thought that decentralization, which often provided rather marginal influence for people at the grass roots, might enhance the regime's legitimacy somewhat by creating modest openings for local sentiments and small opportunities for aspiring but frustrated political activists at low levels. It might facilitate organization-building for the ruling party. It might—as in Côte d'Ivoire—draw local groups into the system "to let the electors do some of the (government's) dirty work" in purging the ruling party of undesirable personnel (Faure, 1989, p. 71)—in that case, in the interests of greater influence of the central leader over his party.

It is a great benefit to decentralization that most politicians did not see it as a means of solving the fiscal problems of central governments—for two main reasons. First, as we shall see in Part VI below, it has made little contribution to local resource mobilization, whatever some theorists may believe. Second, these politicians tended not to off-load too many tasks from central to lower levels without providing the resources to fulfil them—a habit which is deeply damaging to decentralized authorities.

Binswanger and Deininger also assess arguments that fiscal crises can trigger revolts which, in their turn, persuade governments to undertake policy change. This has counted for little in the recent wave of decentralizations. The evidence offers very few examples of this sort of process. We find revolts in Sri Lanka, Colombia and the Philippines. But in all of these cases, these insurrections had their roots in things other than fiscal crises—a point which is recognized in some of the literature (Binswanger and Deininger, 1997). And several governments elsewhere which face revolts have preferred not to decentralize.

Nonetheless, it should be acknowledged that a significant number of governments have decentralized because they were concerned not with imminent revolt, but with discontent among rural (and sometimes urban) dwellers which might ultimately have crystallized into insurgency. A number of them did so on the (often half-understood) assumptions (which were accurate when a substantial devolution of powers and resources occurred) that democratic decentralization could:

- Ease such popular discontents;
- Deflect some discontents onto subnational authorities; and
- Bring those discontents and the people who felt them within official political structures (in the hope that they would not turn antisystemic), and within a moderate and moderating political process of bargaining and representation.

This last point brings us to one further, important theme: institutionalizing decentralization. These words imply not just the creation of such institutions, but their acceptance by both the people whom they serve and by political elites at all levels, especially those in central government who might be tempted to claw back power from them. Such institutionalization is essential if their survival is to be secured. We also need to consider here the potential implications of institutionalization for the future of politics and public policy.

These implications link us to another key concern in the work of Tilly and others—the ways in which political innovations can help foster and sustain creative policies. We are talking here about sustaining decentralized institutions themselves, the creative results of decentralization, and other creative policies and reforms which governments may adopt. Binswanger and Deininger summarize a sizeable literature on various kinds of policy reform when they say that "a politically vocal coalition supporting reform is necessary to ensure that reform is durable and successful" (Binswanger and Deininger, 1997, p. 51).

We noted earlier that no such coalition existed at the grass roots in favor of decentralization prior to the recent wave of devolutions. But the bestowal of *substantial* powers and resources onto elected authorities at lower levels can produce significant benefits to rural dwellers. So we should expect it to generate popular support for decentralization. Indeed, this has already happened (see for example, the chapter on Karnataka in Crook and Manor, 1994). The evidence also indicates, however, that this tends not to protect such devolutions against decisions by higher level politicians to weaken or even to abandon lower level authorities. But it can make that more difficult.

It can also generate changes that enrich the policy process and help to sustain beneficial policies. Binswanger and Deininger note that

"Where potential beneficiaries are not sufficiently organized politically, or where there is little policy-dialogue that allows government to explain and fine-tune its policies, reform programs often encounter great difficulties" (Binswanger and Deininger, 1997, p. 52).

The empirical evidence on serious attempts at decentralization clearly demonstrates its promise here on several fronts. It catalyzes associational activity and the development of organizational capacity among groups at the grass roots. It helps them to learn "lobbying technology" (Becker, 1985). It draws increasing numbers of people and groups into lobbying, bargaining, and political participation more generally—into active engagement with the formal institutions of state, often for the first time. It spawns structures and processes (formal and informal) which facilitate these things. It changes incentive structures for political participation by giving rural dwellers opportunities to exercise influence over decisions that affect their lives.

Decentralization therefore assists—up to a point— in tackling the low collective action potential of small farmers and of other, even poorer groups.[21] It has genuine promise in fostering, over time, a more equitable balance of power both between local communities and higher levels of government, and between more and less prosperous groups within local arenas. Decentralization strengthens civil society (defined here as organized interests with a degree of autonomy from the state). It integrates preexisting, informal arrangements and processes at the local level for managing resources and local affairs into the official political process.

This can enhance the sustainability not just of decentralization but of other creative development policies. Decentralization makes rural dwellers more aware of government policies, and better able to differentiate between those which are beneficial and those which are not. It does so, first, by enhancing transparency—by making it possible for very large numbers of people at lower levels in the political system to see how many resources are available for development and how decisions on their use are being made.

This does not necessarily imply, however, that it guarantees that governments will gain support for painful innovations like structural adjustment programs. It may help, but if the new policies cause great distress, they can put decentralization at risk. This probably explains some of the problems that decentralization encountered in Rawlings' Ghana—although devolution there was managed so cynically that it had little chance of succeeding in any case (Crook and Manor, 1994).

Decentralization also helps ordinary people to develop their analytical capacities, and to make use of them. Overcentralized systems badly need this if policies which take account of local perceptions and needs are to be devised and sustained. Decentralization promotes, mightily, the flow of information (including discontent about policies) from people at lower levels to the upper reaches of government. When that occurs and when government institutions become more responsive— and both things tend to happen when substantial devolution occurs— people at the grass roots become less alienated and they develop a sense of ownership over creative policies which emerge. They therefore become more inclined to sustain both the development projects which result from those policies and the policies themselves.

It is not clear, from present evidence, that decentralization can increase the material resources and the productive capacity of poorer groups in rural populations. It can even, in the short run, make that less likely because local elites often seize most of the advantages which decentralization offers. We shall see presently, however, that these things may change over the longer term.

Some analysts (for example, de Janvry, 1981) argue that the *only* reliable way to achieve an increase in participation and the collective action potential of poorer groups is to increase the resources available to them, through redistributive policies. The empirical evidence suggests that they are mistaken. Poor as well as prosperous people participate more and increase their collective action potential as a result of decentralization—even where it works mainly to the advantage of elites. Over time, the greater transparency offered by democratic systems at lower levels, the increased participation of poorer groups, and their developing skills at influencing those systems may well assist them in curbing the power of rural elites to appropriate benefits. Indeed, in modest ways, this has begun to occur.

These analysts also argue, rightly, that improved education and health services for the rural poor will enhance their ability to participate. Decentralization, on present evidence tends to improve the delivery of education and health services to rural communities generally (with some reservations, noted in Part VI). In time, this may well provide poorer groups as well as their more prosperous neighbours with gains that have positive political implications for them.

Decentralization can also assist in promoting political realism, political stability and a state which is in many ways stronger than in the days of centralized governance. These things are bound up with one another.

First, consider realism. Decentralization increases hugely the numbers of people at lower levels in political systems who know how much public money is available for development. They therefore become more aware of budget constraints. Their interactions with decentralized institutions—even, or *especially*, when they produce modest (and hence politically manageable) frustrations over the limits on resources—yield a rough but realistic understanding of what is and is not possible from government. This promotes political stability. The new realism makes it far less likely that wildly unrealistic expectations of government will develop, and that ordinary people will believe exaggerated promises from politicians. (Not incidentally, this creates disincentives for politicians to make such promises.) All of this protects political systems from the severe backlashes that can occur when inflated expectations prove, inevitably, to be illusory (Manor, 1979).

Decentralization can enhance political stability in at least three other ways. First, by making government institutions more responsive to people at lower levels, it can break down popular cynicism about politics and increase the legitimacy of the political system. Second, by creating a large number of elected posts in authorities at lower levels, it generates opportunities for political activists at those levels who aspire to a role in government. This eases their frustrations which, if left unattended, can threaten stability. Third, it eases the frustrations of opposition parties (and sometimes of interest groups) by increasing the number of arenas in which there are political prizes to be won. After decentralization, elections occur not just to the national presidency or legislature, but to authorities at regional and local levels. This helps to persuade opposition parties and interests, whose candidates lose elections for one of these bodies, to remain engaged with the democratic process, since they may win in another arena at the next opportunity (Jenkins, 1997).

As Binswanger and Deininger observe, there is abundant empirical evidence on "the close relationship between political instability, low private investment and low growth" (Edwards and Tabellini, 1991; Alesina and others, 1993; Edwards, 1994, cited in Binswanger and Deininger, 1997). So greater stability can facilitate economic growth. It can also reduce the need for the state to deploy coercion to maintain order, and strengthen the state's capacity to play noncoercive roles which foster both development and improved state-society relations.

When the state tends increasingly to relate to society in noncoercive ways, as it does when decentralization works well, it gains certain kinds of strength. It inspires greater trust, it acquires greater accommodative capacity, and creative potential for partnerships with society, and others. These things are more than adequate compensations for abandoning commandism. (And remember, doubts about the strength which supposedly flows from commandism have grown since the late 1970s.) These forms of strengthening do not require the state to shed all of its coercive power. It can retain much of this, largely held in abeyance—as indeed it should, in case of disorder. So an increase in noncoercive powers need not be matched by an equal and opposite decrease in coercive potential.

These new kinds of strength both result from and encourage greater accountability—of bureaucrats to elected representatives, and of elected representatives to their constituents. That provides stronger checks on arbitrary and excessive action by state agents, which in turn inspire greater trust, accommodation and the like: a virtuous circle. And, as we have noted, these things make it more likely that creative policies will be sustained by people at the grass roots, and that those people will be more inclined to tolerate and possibly to support new policies which may at first demand sacrifices—provided that they do not suffer too severely.

Notes

1. Huntington included two further propositions which are irrelevant here because they applied to waves of democratization in different eras.

2. Huntington makes a similar point at Huntington, 1992, p. 39.

3. See the chapters on Côte d'Ivoire after 1988 and Ghana in Crook and Manor (1994).

4. Anwar Shah of the World Bank stressed this to me in Entebbe, Uganda, January 13, 1997. For evidence on Brazil, see Tendler (1997, p. 10). For further evidence on cases in Latin America, Africa and Asia see Nickson (1995), and Crook and Manor (1994).

5. Communication from Ole Therkildsen, advisor to the Tanzanian government, March 23, 1997.

6. This was apparent, for example, in the enthusiasm which Scandinavian donors and the Ford Foundation showed in decentralized institutions in Bangladesh and India, after they had come into being.

7. See for example, Crook and Manor (1994, chapter three); and Souza, (1994, pp. 591-92). Also, communication from Ole Therkildsen, advisor to the Tanzanian government, March 23, 1997.

8. I am grateful to William Drennan for help on this case. See Drennan, 1995.

9. Interview with Abdul Nazir Sab, Bangalore, January 11, 1985.

10. For an early discussion of this, see Manor (1981).

11. I am grateful to Surichai Wun'gaeo, Raymond Bryant, and David Potter for evidence of this.

12.. I am grateful to Charles Tripp for help on this point.

13. A similar but less radical reform had actually preceded the Biafra war. It had replaced the four regions inherited from the British period with ten states. The 1976 reform enlarged that number to nineteen.

14. Most governments in francophone Africa created local councils in a few large towns, but they did not develop systems of territorial local government

of the kind known in Commonwealth Africa. Salazar's autocratic regime in Portugal created, on paper at least, local councils in Mozambique and Angola in the very late colonial period. But these had little substance, given the anti-democratic biases of the Salazar government and the problems posed by the guerrilla wars which were raging when the councils were established. I am grateful to Richard Crook for advice on these cases.

15. Latin America is of course a huge, variegated region. But some generalizations are possible, on the understanding that there are a few exceptions to these. Centralization far outweighed decentralization in the period between the Second World War and the early 1980s. This tendency was especially marked in countries ruled by military regimes, but even democratic governments were usually disinclined to decentralize. The emergence of civilian regimes across much of Latin America in and around the early 1980s brought pressure for decentralization, and several regimes responded with new laws and programs to promote this. But the results in practice often disappointed advocates of decentralization (Nickson, 1995, Part 2; and Fox, 1994).

16. I am grateful to John Sidel for help on this point.

17. This entailed, among other things, a redrawing of some provincial boundaries—partly to deal with the rather irrational fragmentation of the country into former areas of white rule and bantustans, and partly to provide ethnic minorities with arenas in which they might exercise some influence and thus feel less alienated (Muthien and Khosa, 1995).

It is worth noting that the predominant aims of this exercise differed from those which have guided other similar processes elsewhere. A comparison with two contrasting cases, which occurred earlier than the period covered by this study, is instructive. Those who revised regional boundaries in India (in and after 1956) and Nigeria (in the 1970s) were both more preoccupied with ethnic divisions than were their South African counterparts. But they proceeded in opposite directions from one another. In India, state borders were redrawn to be roughly congruent with linguistic regions. In Nigeria, they were altered so that they would be incongruent with 'ethnic' divisions, to fragment them. The Nigerians feared that congruence would encourage separatism. The Indians believed that the substantial heterogeneity within linguistic regions would suffice to prevent the new states from becoming the bases for separatist movements. As things turned out, the calculations of both governments on this issue were proved largely correct.

18. For example, in early 1997, the Nigerian regime prepared to hold local elections just when it was facing pressure from the OAU and the Commonwealth over human rights violations, and just when it was filing treason charges against 15 people, including Nobel Laureate Wole Soyinka. Five hand-picked parties were permitted to contest these, and they were sufficiently intimidated by the central authorities that they said next to nothing about issues or policies. Financial Times, March 14, 1997.

19. Interview with P.V. Narasimha Rao, February 11, 1992.

20. It fell flat, mainly because his decentralization proposal was a promise and not a living reality, because he hit on the idea at the very end of his five-year term of office, and because he had governed poorly. But it is not a bad slogan.

21. It is important that we not exaggerate here. Recent advice to President Clinton, about long-standing efforts from above in the U.S. to promote participation, has stressed that substantial efforts were still required to provide training and capacity building among local-level groups. I am grateful to John Gaventa for this information.

●

Part IV
Politics, State-Society Relations, and Decentralization

We now explore some of the complexities which can arise when experiments with decentralization become enmeshed with politics and state-society relations in rural areas. Here, we mainly consider experiments that have some democratic content, because—as we noted in Part I—these qualify as the most common and sustainable efforts, and because administrative or fiscal decentralizations without democratic elements tend to be insulated from society.

Much of the literature on decentralization, especially in English-speaking countries, is the work of economists and specialists in public administration. In the literature on Latin America and francophone Africa, somewhat similar approaches derived from legalistic modes of analysis loom large.[1] Scholars working in these traditions have done much to enhance our understanding, but there is a tendency in their writings to underemphasize and misperceive the motivations and actions of *politicians,* and the *political* (rather than the administrative or legalistic) preoccupations of bureaucrats. Many of them also pay less attention than they should to social contexts and the interaction of decentralized political institutions and social forces. These are serious problems. It is almost always politicians who make the key decisions about decentralization. And they have great influence over the manner in which these initiatives are (or are not) implemented. Even if an experiment with decentralization has little or no democratic content and is almost purely administrative or fiscal—that is, if it largely excludes politicians and social groups at lower levels from influence— it is still politicians higher up who usually decide to craft it in that way. When bureaucrats influence the process of decentralization, their political calculations often loom larger than technocratic imperatives.

Before proceeding further, we need to consider the dissonances that often develop between two sets of views concerning decentralization—since this will help us to understand the different ways in which the issues set out below can be perceived. The first set of views bears the imprint of an administrative mentality, while the second arises from a concern to foster democracy and the vitality of decentralized institutions.

Most politicians and technocrats at higher levels of government tend strongly towards the first set of views. Most elected leaders in decentralized authorities tend towards the second. These dissonances (which are inevitable) can sometimes become so acute that they undermine attempts at decentralization. (When fiscal or administrative decentralization is undertaken, unattended by democratic elements, the dissonances are usually more severe.)

As Blair (1995) has helpfully noted, each of four ideas concerning decentralization can be expressed in two different ways: as part of an administrative mentality, or as part of a democratic way of thinking.

a) *Administrative.* Since regional and local variations (even in relatively homogeneous countries) require flexible approaches to different areas, democratic decentralization can help to facilitate effective planning and implementation at the local level.
   Democratic. People at the grass roots, who understand the particularities of their immediate locality, should have real control over how state policies affecting them are formulated and implemented.
b) *Administrative.* There is a need to cultivate political support for the regime at local and intermediate levels (or among elites there), and democratic decentralization can provide patronage channels that will help to achieve that.
   Democratic. Grass roots support for the regime is best generated through mechanisms of accountability, and government should be accountable at or near the local level.
c) *Administrative.* To prevent regional disaffection and secession movements, a bestowal of some autonomy on elected bodies at intermediate and/or local levels is advisable.
   Democratic. The geographical heterogeneity of cultures can fruitfully be accommodated through democratic decentralization.
d) *Administrative.* Responsibilities for service delivery (and sometimes the task of raising funding for it) can be transferred from the national level downward through decentralization, easing burdens on the central government.
   Democratic. Publicly funded local services are more effectively provided when people at intermediate and/or local levels can influence the process.

The dissonance between these two outlooks can create severe problems when central authorities pursue their ends very aggressively, or when they overreact to the discoveries that not all of their assumptions are accepted at the grass roots, and that not all of their expectations are realistic. If leaders in central government can be made more aware of the perceptions which tend to develop within decentralized institutions, and if their expectations can be scaled down, they may not needlessly undermine systems which hold real promise—both for rural development and for the leaders themselves. Let us now turn to some of the issues that arise when decentralization encounters political and social forces.

Conditions for Success: Crucial and Merely Helpful

Let us begin by considering an array of things which help experiments with democratic decentralization succeed. Four items qualify as crucial conditions. None is sufficient on its own to produce success. All are vitally important—indeed, in the absence of any one of them, failure is probable. All four are things that are internal to government and to decentralized systems.[2] This may suggest that they have more to do with administration than with politics. But all arise because politicians make politically motivated decisions on the content of reforms.

It is crucial that decentralized systems have:

- Sufficient powers to exercise substantial influence within the political system and over significant development activities;
- Sufficient financial resources to accomplish important tasks;
- Adequate administrative capacity to accomplish those tasks; and
- Reliable accountability mechanisms—to ensure both the accountability of elected politicians to citizens, and the accountability of bureaucrats to elected politicians.

Recent research (Crook and Manor, 1994) indicates that accountability mechanisms are the most important of these four elements, but all are crucial.

A number of other conditions are less than crucial, but their presence is quite helpful. It is especially helpful if a country has had some experience of democracy at higher levels prior to decentralization. Sustained experience with this acquaints both elected politicians and bureaucrats with the idea that the latter should be accountable to the former. It acquaints everyone with the idea that elected politicians should be accountable to citizens, and that government has obligations to the people. (The latter idea is not nearly so widely accepted as is often supposed.) It enables large numbers of political activists to develop skills at making a success of the politics of representation, coalition building, bargaining, and so on. It often provides citizens with a realistic set of expectations about what open government can and cannot achieve. Democracies also tend to provide considerable freedom for the press, which is also helpful to the workings of democratic decentralization.

Two other important and closely related factors are the existence of a lively civil society and the availability of social capital. It is nearly always helpful to have the former. (There is a huge literature on "civil society," but let us define it here simply as "organized interests with a significant degree of autonomy from the state.") The words "nearly always" are worth noting, since very occasionally, organized interests can be lively in severely conflictual ways which make it more, not less, difficult for decentralized authorities to work creatively.

The term "social capital" refers to the density of interactions within and among social groups and voluntary associations, which generate mutual trust that can facilitate public activity. This is a concept developed by James Coleman and famously elaborated by Robert Putnam (Putnam, and others, 1993). This is closely related to a lively civil society, but it is not the same thing.

There is little doubt that when these two things are present, they almost always tend to assist decentralized authorities to work well. But the presence of these two factors is not sufficient to ensure the success of decentralization, since if a system lacks resources, accountability, and so on, it will founder. And it is not necessary to have either of these things on hand to enable decentralized institutions to function creatively.

Some readers have expressed doubts that decentralization can achieve much in the absence of these two things, especially a lively civil society. To reassure them, let us briefly consider four points.

First, when elected authorities at lower levels are established, their members tend to act quickly and forcefully to undertake projects which they think the people who voted for them desire—whether or not civil society is vibrant. In that early phase, they do not need energetic advice from organized interests to identify at least a few much-needed innovations which will be widely welcomed. Such innovations are usually obvious.

Second, those elected representatives need no coaching from civil society to understand that they must assert themselves in their dealings with bureaucrats. It is again obvious that this is an urgent priority. The problem in that initial phase is typically that these representatives act too aggressively, not too timidly, towards bureaucrats.

Third, we need to consider the setting in which such actions occur. Before decentralization, bureaucrats were nearly always far less responsive to or aware of the views of local groups than they become once it occurs. And most governments were so preoccupied with grand, centralized undertakings that they neglected (often grossly) the kind of small-scale but badly needed initiatives which decentralized authorities almost always undertake. The psychological impact of just a few such small-scale projects is usually quite considerable, since they appear to be (and generally are) radical departures from the near-vacuum that often preceded them. So in that first phase after decentralization, the creation of representative institutions alone suffices to get the new system off to a promising start—even in the absence of a lively civil society, or indeed, abundant social capital.

Finally, that psychological impact swiftly catalyzes greater participation and associational activity among interests at lower levels. So civil society soon emerges to begin to play a creative role in such systems. This happens not just where civil society is sluggishly active, but even where it has long been systematically repressed by the state. An example of such an extreme case was Côte d'Ivoire in the mid-1980s (Crook, 1991; Crook and Manor, 1994). It should be clear from all of this that decentralization usually produces entirely adequate achievements in the absence of a lively civil society—and it does not remain absent for long.

Unfounded Assertions about "Preconditions" for Successful Decentralization

We sometimes hear voices from both the left and the right claim that decentralization cannot work in the absence of certain preconditions which suit their tastes. These need to be treated with extreme caution, since they tend to be unfounded. Two examples will illustrate the point.

Land reform. It is common to hear people from the Indian state of West Bengal—where the Communist Party of India-Marxist governments since 1977 have developed impressive decentralized institutions—say that success is impossible unless serious land reform precedes decentralization. Prior land reform helps facilitate success, but it is patently not essential. Such institutions have also worked well in areas where land reform has made little headway, such as neighbouring Bangladesh or the Indian state of Karnataka. This is, of course, not to deny that disputes over land control will sometimes surface as heated issues within lower level arenas once decentralization occurs. There is evidence from, for example, Mali, to indicate that this can happen (Evers, 1994, p. 31; Hessling and Ba, 1994). But this does not mean that land reform must take place before decentralization.

Market orientation and private sector development. Consider, by contrast, a World Bank document which alleges that an "effective and broad market orientation and private sector development" are crucial "preconditions" for successful decentralization. The same document claims that "another essential process" is "the emergence and development of entrepreneurial middle classes" (Fuhr, p. 2). Once again, such things are helpful (unless private sector development is attended by the rise of extreme inequalities or severe social conflict, or both). But even when the state has loomed large in the economy, decentralized authorities have functioned well and provided, among others, greater accountability and responsiveness from governments. And in numerous societies where the middle classes are badly underdeveloped—and in rural arenas where it is difficult to find more than handful of people whom we could describe as middle class, decentralization has yielded similar benefits. If we waited either for significant land reform or for the emergence of a strong market economy before decentralizing, we would miss opportunities to make creative changes in a very large number of countries.

Importance of Historical Legacies

The inheritance from the past has a powerful impact on politics and social dynamics in the present, and can either impede or facilitate decentralization. Preexisting political traditions count for much here. In Africa and Asia, the varied legacies of colonial regimes matter greatly. They inspire either continuity or rejection from their successors.

The British imperial penchant for local councils, usually elected on a first-past-the-post basis, has inspired plenty of each. French colonial regimes did less decentralizing, and both they and their successors in Africa have operated according to distinctive principles which impart centralist tendencies to recent decentralized systems there. One of these—the notion of *unicite de caisse* (the unity of the exchequer)—implies that resources raised by local authorities should go into a national revenue pool. Those authorities sometimes have difficulty persuading central governments to release funds on demand. Another—the concept of *cumul des mandats* (the accumulation of mandates)—encourages leaders of local authorities simultaneously to seek and hold offices at the national level. That inclines them to a preoccupation with national rather than local affairs and priorities.

When the Americans took over the Philippines, they rushed to organize elections of mayors all across the archipelago, *before* they had constructed bureaucratic agencies at, or reaching down to, the local level. (In so doing, they reversed the sequencing seen in the French and British

Empires, where bureaucracies were in place long before democratization.) The result was that Filipino mayors developed their own local bureaucracies and packed them with their friends and relatives—creating a system of local bossism which survives to this day. These sorts of legacies clearly need to be understood if we are to grasp how decentralization might work in such varied contexts.

We also need to look at the failures, the successes, or the complete absence of prior experiments with decentralization in these places. Also important are certain elements of indigenous political culture—Gandhian traditions in India which facilitate decentralization, and the Chinese fear of "localism" (a word which implies assertiveness not only at the grass roots, but in regions as well)—which impedes it.

Varied experiences of commandism and centralization also need to be considered. The failure of authoritarian regimes in Latin America in the 1970s to produce economic growth inoculated people there against the notion that autocracy is economically productive.[3] Commandism can also entail attempts to repress civil society which create problems for decentralization. But the more liberal commandism of the Nehru years encouraged civil society to flourish in India—something which partly explains the success of decentralization in some states there. The presence or absence of multiparty systems, press freedoms, and so on—which are part of these countries' inheritance—also create opportunities and problems for decentralization. An in-depth understanding of such factors is essential when decentralization is assessed in any setting.

Virtues of Simplicity

The importance of simplicity and clarity in institutional arrangements needs to be stressed. Excessively simple schemes are dangerous. But the greater worry is excessive complexity and elaboration, which can breed confusion—especially if (as often happens) interested parties (such as high-level politicians or bureaucrats who fear a loss of power) find it convenient to sow confusion in order to weaken decentralized systems. Elaborate arrangements may seem the way to achieve high ideals, but the best may turn out to be the enemy of the good.

In the Indian state of Karnataka, for example, two severely disadvantaged groups (the scheduled castes and scheduled tribes) have seats on local and intermediate-level councils reserved for them in proportion to their numerical strength—usually around 22 percent of the population. (All voters cast ballots in elections for such seats, but only members of these groups may stand for office.) Additionally, not less than one-third of the seats in all councils are reserved for women, and another third are reserved for groups called the "backward classes."

These groups stand above the severely disadvantaged scheduled castes in the traditional hierarchy, so that they occupy the middle levels on the status ladder.

The complications do not end there, however. The backward classes are divided into group A (consisting of relatively more backward groups) for which 80 percent of their one-third of the seats are reserved, and group B (less backward groups) to which 20 percent are allocated. And to complicate things still further, the posts of chairs and vice-chairs of all councils are also reserved for these various groups in these varying proportions, on a rotating basis every few years. The result is a thicket of complexities which may produce more confusion than justice. Architects of decentralization need to avoid such over-elaboration if it is at all possible.

Jealousy of Power Holders at Higher Levels

Most politicians everywhere are mainly preoccupied with maintaining and enhancing their own influence. Few are able to grasp the subtlety that even though decentralization deprives them of some powers, it can reinforce their influence in more important ways. It can, for example, empower them by greatly enhancing the flow of information from government to society and, especially, from society to government. It can (crucially) mightily enhance the responsiveness of government. These and other gains from decentralization bolster the legitimacy of both the leaders and the political system more generally. (For enlarged and creative roles which high-level politicians can play in decentralized systems, see below.)

Unfortunately, most politicians fix on the influence which they lose through devolution. In 1988, one quite enlightened member of the cabinet in the Indian state of Karnataka (an unusually successful experiment) complained that "I am the Minister of Education, but I cannot decide on the location of a school in my own constituency—the *Zilla Parishad* (District Council) does that now."[4]

When they see such things happening, many politicians try to claw back the power passed to decentralized bodies, and they are often assisted by high-level bureaucrats who share their sentiments. This is especially likely when changes of government at higher levels occur (but not only then). In an election in the Indian state of Maharashtra in 1995, for example, the Shiv Sena and the Bharatiya Janata Party ousted the Congress Party from power. They found the elected bodies at lower levels dominated by the Congress and promptly set about depriving them of powers and resources.[5]

This sort of jealousy is the greatest (and an omnipresent) threat to decentralization. It has wrecked many promising experiments. This has occurred for example not only in Ghana, where the promise of decentralization was open to doubt, but also in Bangladesh and some Indian states where its potential was beyond dispute (Crook and Manor, 1994). There is not much that can be done about it, other than to try to prepare high-level power holders for the loss of powers which will attend decentralization, and to explain the more subtle and substantial gains that will accrue to them if they can tolerate those losses.

For useful ideas on how central governments can play more creative roles in making decentralization work well—and, in the process, become less antagonistic to decentralization—see the section below "Mistakes at Higher Levels." See also, "Popular Pressure for Decentralization" below on approaches which may ensure greater consultation between elected members of decentralized councils and their constituents.

Other Reasons for Intrusions from Higher Levels

The tendency of powerful people in central governments to act in ways that damage decentralization is attributable to more than their appetites for power. Even those who are sympathetic to decentralization can be moved to intervene when they find that events are unfolding in unanticipated, disturbing ways.

This often happens because the expectations which senior politicians and bureaucrats had of decentralization turn out to be inaccurate and naively optimistic. Such naiveté can take many forms. (These problems are discussed in great detail in Part VI of this paper, but they are worth a brief mention here.)

It is common for architects of decentralization to overestimate the ability and inclination of decentralized authorities to engage effectively in planning exercises from below. When no coherent plans emerge, or when plans consist of local politicians' ill-conceived wish lists—as they often do—people higher up tend to react with astonishment and dismay. They often have similar reactions to unexpected problems with monitoring and evaluation. This can take two forms. Power holders at higher levels may discover that they are far less able than they had hoped to monitor and evaluate the doings of decentralized authorities. They may also find that those authorities are far less able or willing to monitor and evaluate projects which they initiate, or that they are unable or disinclined to convey their evaluations (especially of failures) to higher-ups.

Those at the apex of a political system may also suffer disappointment over the incapacity—or again, and more crucially here, the disinclination—of decentralized bodies to mobilize local resources. Newly elected leaders of local or regional councils may prefer not to levy fresh taxes or to press for more efficient collection of existing taxes because they fear that this will make them unpopular. They may prefer to make do with the funds provided from above.

Higher-ups may also be surprised and distressed at the limited capacity of decentralized bodies to implement even slightly complicated development projects—even when the administrative machinery available to such bodies is so insubstantial that this should come as no surprise. This problem can be especially acute when central leaders see their own programs poorly implemented by decentralized agencies.

The same reaction can occur when those at the apex of a system see decentralized authorities diverting resources from areas dear to the hearts of central leaders, in order to pursue their own rather different agendas. Things like this reinforce the inclination of high-level leaders to give way to their jealousy towards decentralized bodies, and to seek to claw back powers and resources that have been devolved.

Mistakes at Higher Levels

Some of the unwelcome surprises which await high-level leaders when decentralization occurs, result from their own misjudgments in designing decentralization schemes. They may provide decentralized authorities with inadequate funds and administrative resources—or, from their point of view, with too much of these things. They may concentrate too intensely on framing watertight bureaucratic rules and controls, and not on the more important business of creating structures within which open politics can flourish—thus strangling the new institutions at birth. They may create broad legal frameworks for decentralized institutions without then developing the regulations and initiatives to implement them (Shah and Qureshi, 1994). They may fail in the (admittedly difficult) task of crafting effective devices to ensure accountability. They may promise more to decentralized bodies than they can realistically deliver. Or they may promise them little other than headaches by treating decentralization mainly as a means of off-loading onerous responsibilities while cutting expenditures.

Giving Central Governments More Creative Roles in Making Decentralization Work Well

Judith Tendler has recently identified several ways in which central governments can help decentralized systems to function well. Since she proposes a more powerful and visible role for central institutions, her suggestions can ease the antagonism which many high-level politicians feel towards decentralization and which is a major danger to it.

Tendler anchors her work in a criticism of the literature on development which, she argues, fixes excessively on self-interest and rent-seeking as motivations for government employees' behaviour. She quotes Charles Sabel's view that much recent social science is a "science of suspicion. It makes the pursuit of self-interest and the fear of deception...the spring of individual action and the guiding motive of institutional construction" (Sabel, 1997, quoted in Tendler 1997). Sabel reminds us of Talleyrand's comment that "the most suspicious people make the biggest dupes" (Sabel, 1997).

Tendler prefers to draw upon the literature on industrial performance and workplace transformation, which stresses initiatives which provide employees with greater job satisfaction and which inspire both dedication to their work and trust between them and users of the services that they provide. Her research focuses on a remarkably successful set of policy initiatives in northeast Brazil. The government there fostered a sense of pride and commitment among its employees who were providing services in new, local-level programs

> with repeated demonstrations of admiration and respect for what they were doing. It built a sense of calling around these particular programs and their workers. It publicized the programs incessantly, even their minor successes. It gave prizes for good performance, with much pomp and ceremony....When it recruited and trained workers for some of these programs, it talked to them like a chosen people (Tendler, 1997, pp. 136–37).

All this contributed to a new

> respect for these workers by the public—remarkable in a time of widespread contempt for government. Workers revelled in the new respect and, in a kind of virtuous circle, they wanted to live up to it. Note the difference in this sequence of improved performance from that implicit in development advice, where the public servant is presumed guilty of self-interest unless proven otherwise (Tendler, 1997, pp. 136–37).

The sustained publicity campaign which the government mounted also created popular enthusiasm for the politicians higher up who created the programs—something which will appeal to high-level leaders everywhere—but there was more to it than that. Employees carried out more and more varied tasks than is common in most such settings. These included "the brokering of connections between clients and the larger world of government agencies and private suppliers." This gave them greater job satisfaction and

> cohered together in a client-centric, problem-solving approach to service delivery. It gave rise to trusting and respectful relationships between clients and public servants (Tendler, 1997, p. 138).

This approach also persuaded people at the grass roots to monitor program implementation and to protest when government employees performed badly. It encouraged local interests and nongovernmental organizations to play active roles in influencing programs, so that they conformed more to local preferences and were adapted to local conditions (Tendler 1997, pp. 140–41).

Tendler rightly stresses that her findings imply the need for decentralizing governments to continue playing centralized roles even as they devolve power. But the evidence amassed in the present study suggests that she carries this too far, into an unnecessarily negative judgment on the promise of decentralization. It makes more sense to consider incorporating the approaches which she suggests into experiments with decentralization.

This could serve several useful purposes. Consider two examples. It could encourage nonofficial associations to engage more actively with decentralized institutions and persuade citizens that local governance is not the sole territory of the elected local council (de los Reyes and Jopillo, 1995). It could also reassure central leaders by giving them an important role, even as it encouraged both the dedication of government employees and the active involvement of people at the grass roots.

Also note, in connection with the section below on the uses of participatory rural appraisal techniques, that such techniques require sustained intervention from atop political systems to ensure that they are implemented and understood (Gaventa, 1997).

The Danger of Inflating Popular Expectations

We saw earlier how the unrealistic expectations of high-level politicians and bureaucrats can threaten decentralization. The same can be said of inflated expectations among citizens. A government that undertakes decentralization is naturally inclined to speak in glowing terms about its promise. They would be well-advised, however, to exercise restraint here, lest ordinary people anticipate too much.

Our evidence indicates that the people tend to anticipate a lot even without official encouragement. This is closely bound up with their eagerness for small-scale development projects which have usually received less attention from higher levels of government than villagers wish. However much decentralized bodies may seek to respond to this, they may not be able to deliver enough, quickly enough to satisfy popular appetites.

We should understand that people at the grass roots seldom have a realistic understanding of the limitations on what decentralized bodies can achieve. If a decentralized system functions tolerably well for a sustained period, many citizens will eventually acquire such an understanding (Manor, 1979). But in the early stages, when the system is most vulnerable to the jealousy of higher-ups, this problem needs to be anticipated, lest the new system lose popular legitimacy. One way of easing this problem is to provide plentiful resources to decentralized bodies, but that is often difficult if governments are hard pressed for funds and especially if they see decentralization (wrongly) as a means of cutting overall expenditure.

Attracting Responsible Leaders and Combating Clientelism

Bureaucrats the world over, together with high-level politicians and specialists in public administration, often complain about the types of people who come to power in elected authorities when democratic decentralization takes place. They regard many of these people as unlettered, rustic, inexperienced, corrupt and so preoccupied with their small bailiwicks that they are blind to the larger concerns which animate those at higher levels in the system. They seek approaches to facilitate the emergence of "better" mayors, councillors, and others, in decentralized systems.[6] Many of these approaches entail the creation of elaborate sets of administrative rules. These solve little and usually create trouble because they are bureaucratic solutions to what are essentially political problems.

The anxieties which these people express often call attention to the problem of clientelism, that is, the tendency of leaders to get themselves elected by using networks of clients to whom they then show inordinate favoritism once in office. A certain amount of such behaviour is inevitable, indeed it is—up to a point—democracy in action and needs to be seen as such. But it can also be a genuine problem.

When it is, it would help if decentralizers everywhere would emulate their counterparts across much of Latin America (Nickson, 1995) in recognizing that the best (if imperfect) solution to this political problem is itself political. If fair elections are held at regular intervals, the poor performance of politicians who carry clientelism to excess or who behave irresponsibly in other ways will often ensure their defeat. Since politicians are preoccupied with gaining and retaining power, most of them will eventually see that such forms of irresponsibility can hit them where it hurts most, and they or others will develop more responsible modes of governance. This was apparent, for example, in Bangladesh after 1985 (Crook and Manor, 1994).

Fine Line between Clientelism and More Creative, Institutionalized Patronage Systems

When systems of patron-client ties develop within democratic institutions—as they usually do, at least to a limited degree—worries naturally develop about clientelism. It is important that we recognize, however, that not all of the systems which politicians in decentralized authorities develop to distribute patronage (goods and services) to groups from whom they need support qualify as nefarious clientelism.

Such systems may be highly personalized—and in authorities located at or near the local level where everyone knows everyone else, that is hardly surprising. But many of the more successful ones—which often ensure leaders' reelection—acquire a more institutionalized character. That is to say, they are focused less on assisting the leader's small circle of cronies and more on reaching an array of social groups who can ensure his political survival. When that happens, the leader seeks to reach certain *types* of people rather than certain known individuals, and becomes preoccupied with impersonal policies that assist those groups rather than personalized handouts. There is a fine line between clientelism and this more constructive type of patronage politics, but we need to look for the subtle differences between these things, lest we dismiss much that is creative in the doings of elected leaders.

Creating Formal Structures with Politics and Accountability as the Main Concerns

Despite the comments in the preceding two sections, we also need to recognize that formal rules and structures do matter. This is true even in countries where laws and constitutions are often disregarded. In such countries, politicians in decentralized institutions have to wage informal battles to secure at least some of the powers which the formal laws promise them, and to ensure that bureaucrats remain as accountable to elected representatives as the formal structures require. But the existence of those formal provisions improves their chances of success. In such countries, organized interests have to wage informal battles to ensure that politicians in decentralized authorities remain as account-able to citizens as the formal structures require, but again, the existence of those formal provisions simplifies their task (see for example, World Bank, 1995, pp. 9 and 13).

The key requirements wherever laws and rules are devised are to make them as unambiguous as possible, to construct them on the under-standing that it is politics and not bureaucratic regulation that mainly matters in democratic systems, and to craft them in ways that maximize the chances for two kinds of accountability to be achieved. These are first, the accountability of bureaucrats to elected politicians and, second, the accountability (frequently and fairly) of politicians to citizens.

Deconcentration and Devolution—Problem of Sequencing

Decentralizers who are considering the devolution of powers and resources onto elected authorities at intermediate or local levels, or both, need to ask whether people working for line ministries that pro-mote development have previously been deconcentrated to those lev-els. If this has already occurred, it has two major benefits.

First, it means that the development bureaucracy will need little or no restructuring or enlargement. This makes the process of decentralization easier, cheaper and more likely to succeed. If bureaucratic agencies need to be deconcentrated at the same time as devolution occurs, this greatly complicates things. If it is neglected or done inadequately or funded insufficiently, decentralized authorities will have major difficulties accomplishing things. If numerous new hirings of bureaucrats are required, this can increase both the cost of decentralization and the risk that inexperienced and ill-qualified staff will cripple the new institutions.

Decentralization and Fiscal Discipline

Some economists have voiced anxieties that decentralization may erode fiscal discipline and central governments' capacity for adequate macro-economic management (Prud'homme, 1995; Tanzi, 1996). To address these concerns, it is useful to distinguish between two types of decen-tralization—one which occurs within federal systems when power and resources are devolved only onto the state or provincial level, and one which entails devolution to still lower levels, closer to the grass roots.

There is some evidence to indicate that decentralization within federal systems may occasionally cause problems. The devolution of much of the power over investment decisions to provincial governments in China is said by some, though not all, commentators to have produced macro-economic imbalances and inflationary pressures (Naughton, 1995).

And yet even if this view is accurate, this case appears to be an exception that proves the contrary rule. Anwar Shah has noted a number of cases in which fiscal decentralization to provincial levels correlates with welcome trends, in macroeconomic management and much more (Shah, 1996).

Or consider the case of India. In recent years spending by state governments has triggered anxieties among officials in the national finance ministry about their ability to keep the overall government deficit down. But the mechanisms which India's and most other national governments have to curb spending at the state level usually suffice to minimize this problem. Indeed, in India, we see state governments developing new strategies which hold considerable promise for improvements in macroeconomic management. The most striking, if little known, example of this is the tax reform program of the Rajasthan government, which entails both the simplification of the tax system and a reduction in some tax rates—which has led to higher revenue collections.[7] The anxieties over the dangers of decentralization within federal systems are overstated.

There is much less reason to worry that decentralization to still lower levels will cause difficulties. It is argued elsewhere in this study that central governments should consider at least modest increases in spending on these lower level institutions, especially in the early phases after decentralization is undertaken. This is helpful in enabling these institutions to break down popular cynicism which in many countries has built up over long periods when government has achieved very little. But we are talking here about relatively small amounts of money, and in any case, officials in national finance ministries usually retain control over how much is committed to this purpose.

Lower level institutions are very unlikely to possess either the power or the inclination to increase public spending by very much. The evidence on decentralization worldwide clearly indicates that it is highly unusual for those institutions to be granted substantial tax-raising powers by central governments—indeed, they often have none at all. And even when they are empowered to impose at least modest taxes, elected representatives in those institutions are (as we note in the section just below) exceedingly reluctant to do so since this will make them unpopular with voters. When they have substantial powers, they often tend to exercise them quite carefully—in, for example, the Philippines where "conservative fiscal management practices" have prevailed (de los Reyes and Jopillo, 1995, p. 88).

Indeed, there is evidence from Central Europe to suggest that democratic decentralization may make a positive contribution to programs of economic liberalization and macroeconomic stabilization in general, and to the success of austerity programs that are aimed at curbing inflation in particular.[8] It is impossible on present evidence to prove a causal connection. But it appears that serious efforts by certain post-Communist governments there to promote democratic decentalization have helped to erode popular disenchantment with government in general, so that citizens became more inclined to tolerate the pain of austerity programs and to accept official explanations of the need for such programs than they would otherwise have been.

Local Resource Mobilization and the Reluctance of Politicians at Lower Levels to Impose Fresh Taxes

This is not a new problem, but it remains a potent reality (Riggs, 1963). Decentralizers—particularly those who see decentralization as a means of reducing central government expenditure, or those who are eager to use it as a device for mobilizing local resources—should anticipate a strong reluctance among elected members of decentralized authorities to levy fresh taxes. These people naturally wish to maintain or enhance their popularity, and they are vividly aware of the reluctance of their constituents to pay additional taxes. They often achieve office thanks to the support of elites in their bailiwicks, and they know that it is mainly the elites who possess the resources which might be tapped through taxation. This makes them doubly reluctant to impose new taxes.

This problem never goes away, but it is especially acute early in the life span of decentralized authorities. If they are given the resources from central government in that initial phase to enable them to achieve useful things, they have a chance to convince their constituents that they have tangible promise. Once that idea takes root—often in places where people have good reason for cynicism about government institutions (and paying taxes)—the authorities will be in a better position to impose taxes, on the understanding that this will make further accomplishments possible. They will also be better able to create conditions that encourage private investment—in profit-making enterprises which hold promise to eventually increase local revenues (World Bank, 1997a), and in local development funds which may emerge out of cofinancing initiatives from higher levels of government. But even then, elected members of these bodies should not be expected to shed their hesitations about imposing fresh levies.

Do Not Expect Rural Taxpayers to Vote with Their Feet

One old chestnut in discussions of decentralization needs to be set aside in any analysis of the developing countries and Eastern Europe—especially one like ours which focuses mainly on rural areas. This is Tiebout's argument that decentralized authorities overseeing various local jurisdictions will compete by offering different standards of services and by imposing different tax burdens—and that taxpayers will vote with their feet in favor of more attractive authorities (Tiebout, 1956).

Others have observed that this has little relevance in developing countries—especially in rural areas (for example, Bardhan, 1997). People there are often less mobile, and when they do move in numbers, it tends strongly to be for extreme reasons such as environmental devastation or the outbreak of epidemics. The evidence on which this study is based offers not a single example to corroborate Tiebout's model. This is explained in large part by two things. First, in the real world, decentralized authorities usually lack significant tax-raising powers. Second, even when they possess them, they are reluctant to court unpopularity by imposing fresh taxes. As a consequence, marked differences in tax rates and resulting service provisions tend not to develop. Tiebout's model should therefore be disregarded here.

Grants from Above Do Not Necessarily Imply Control

Many commentators—especially those who focus mainly on formal rules and arrangements—tend to believe that if decentralized authorities are heavily dependent for resources on grants from higher levels of government, people higher up will necessarily control those authorities. This is seldom true. We should not equate financial dependence with control.

Politicians in decentralized bodies are far more able than is usually supposed to exercise autonomy—by *informal* means, including (often creative) concealment. Given the limitations on the mobilization of local resources, a significant element of funding from above is inevitable in most decentralized systems. If higher level authorities maintain the stability of funding for decentralized bodies, the latter are often able to function effectively, accountably, responsively and largely as they please. Decentralizers should concentrate on providing stable funding and on ensuring that mechanisms exist to facilitate accountability. They should also seek to promote the formal autonomy of decentralized bodies, so that this can be achieved within the rules and not (as will usually happen) by stealth.

Decentralized Authorities' Bias towards Small-Scale Infrastructure Projects

Elected members of decentralized bodies tend strongly to emphasize small-scale building projects—roads, school buildings, bridges, irrigation works, and the like. (Note, however, that a recent multinational enquiry by United States Agency for International Development found important exceptions to this statement in Latin America.[9]) They are often condemned for this and accused of preferring such works because they lend themselves to kickbacks from contractors. There is some substance to this charge, but it is nothing like as simple as that.

Decentralized authorities have several other, less objectionable reasons for this bias. Many of them derive special satisfaction from creating something tangible, to which they can point as evidence of their creativity—not only to voters, but to their family and friends as well. Many of them prefer to commit resources to relatively simple, straightforward projects rather than to more complex innovations in service delivery. They also tend to have rather limited administrative resources, which can manage these simpler matters, but which may not be equal to more complex undertakings.

Finally and not least, their preference for small-scale infrastructure projects tends to be shared by most of their constituents—as systematic surveys of villagers views have demonstrated (Crook and Manor, 1994). However beneficial large-scale development programs may have been, rural dwellers tend to have a rather different conception of what constitutes "rural development." They are enthusiastic about efforts to look after the little things that have been ignored for a very long time.

Decentralized Authorities' Foreshortened Time Perspective

The people who get elected to decentralized authorities—especially at or near the local level—tend to be preoccupied with relatively short time spans.[10] This happens partly because they are not schooled (as industrialists, economists and technocrats usually are) in devising initiatives that extend over longer periods, and partly because they often feel driven to show concrete results to voters in time for an early election. This can cause policymakers higher up in a system frustration, since it sets up a dissonance between the views and programs of people at different levels. But it makes sense in the eyes of these leaders at lower levels, and if democratic decentralization is to succeed, their perspectives need to be treated with some respect.

It is worth stressing that politicians atop political systems are not immune from foreshortened time perspectives. They can also be impatient for quick political payoffs from decentralization, which can be damaging to fledgling authorities at lower levels. Witness, for example, the temperamental reaction of one genuine enthusiast for decentralization, Chief Minister Digvijay Singh of the Indian state of Madhya Pradesh, when the new decentralized system's teething troubles were explained to him.[11]

Need for Patience with Elected Representatives and Voters in Newly Democratized Systems

Policy specialists in donor agencies and people at higher levels in newly democratized countries that have undertaken decentralization need to be patient with elected members of decentralized authorities and with the voters that elect them. The reluctance to impose taxes, the bias towards infrastructure, the foreshortened time perspective mentioned above may cause dismay.

So may a number of other things that are more or less inevitable in countries which are emerging from autocratic phases. It will take time for elected representatives to grasp that in the new system, they are accountable to voters. They may at first behave in the autocratic manner of power holders in the old system. Voters may, for a time, be disorganized, naive and easily gulled. It will take time for political parties to organize themselves so that they can provide voters with clearer choices than are available in the first, often chaotic and rather personalized elections.

Many of these things—especially those in the paragraph just above—are likely to change over time (see for example, Gazaryan and Jeleniewski, 1996). Impatience can destroy the considerable promise of decentralization.

Decentralizing in Uncongenial Social Contexts

This paper is broadly supportive of decentralization. But it is unwise to attempt it in places where conflicts between social groups are especially severe, or where disparities between rich and poor are unusually extreme. Where either is true, it is exceedingly difficult to make decentralization work even tolerably well. Both of these conditions often exist together, and when they do, it is almost certainly naive to expect decentralization to succeed.

Consider, for example, the case of India where the Constitution (since 1993) requires the government of every state to undertake decentralization. This has worked and is working well in a few states where social conflict is not severe and where state governments have been serious about empowering decentralized bodies. It could work well in most states, if governments would be more generous in devolving powers and resources. But no matter what the government in the state of Bihar might do, the extreme economic disparities and social turmoil that exist there are bound to wreck any undertaking—as is currently happening.

Decentralization as an Agent of Social Change

Decentralization should not be expected to generate significant social change—in places afflicted by severe conflict, or even in relatively untroubled places. Decentralized authorities become arenas within which existing social forces manifest themselves and contend politically. In these arenas, conflicts within society acquire a new, political dimension and in the process, they often grow sharper. When poorer groups become better organized and acquire greater "lobbying technology" and other skills, more prosperous groups tend to react aggressively.[12]

It is possible that over time, decentralized institutions can also become arenas within which political bargains and accommodations develop, so that conflicts moderate. And as less prosperous and powerful groups develop a better understanding of how to turn the decentralized system to their advantage, they may make gains. But the available evidence suggests that this will be a very slow process. To expect decentralization to promote substantial social change anytime soon—or to help to pacify a society which is wracked with such severe inequality and conflict that decentralization will probably fail—is naive.

Transparency: Not an Unmixed Blessing

Greater transparency in the workings of government institutions contributes to enhanced accountability. Both of these things rightly find a place in most definitions of good government. Democratic decentralization tends to produce greater transparency. This is, on the whole, a constructive change, but we need to recognize two potential difficulties that can arise from it.

The first is more relevant to the performance of state institutions at higher levels than to decentralized bodies, but it could conceivably have some impact upon the latter as well—although no evidence for this has emerged during this study. A recent study of the political management of economic reforms in India indicates that the Narasimha Rao government succeeded in liberalizing partly because it could "soften the edge of political conflict (which might have arisen from the reforms) by promoting change amidst the appearance of continuity." Its success, which international development agencies that have "good government" agendas applaud, owed much to concealment rather than to transparency (Jenkins, 1997). In this connection, Jenkins recalls Albert O. Hirschman's findings that land reformers often had to rely on "the use of ambiguity and obfuscation" in pursuing their ends.[13] The greater transparency of decentralized, democratic institutions makes it much more difficult for politicians in them to use such tactics for reformist purposes, should they wish to do so.

That may seem a loss only in theory, and perhaps it is. But another problem for decentralized authorities is very real. Transparency is supposed to enhance the legitimacy of political institutions, and it often does so in many ways. But it can also, simultaneously, produce the opposite result, even when this is not justified by events.

The creation of elected district and local councils in the Indian state of Karnataka in the late 1980s, and the devolution of resources and responsibilities onto those councils, caused the overall amount of corruption in the political system to decline. And yet, most villagers believed that corruption had increased because it was now far more visible in the more transparent decentralized system than it had been before. This misperception acted as a counterweight to their tendency to regard the decentralized system as more legitimate than the one which preceded it. That decentralized system was quite successful, so that it was not greatly damaged by this. But in other cases, where decentralized institutions achieve less—which is to say, in most decentralized systems—this sort of thing could prove deeply damaging. There is little that can be done about this, but analysts and advocates of decentralization need to be aware of the problem.

Political Parties and Decentralized Bodies

We often hear it said that political parties should be prevented from taking part in elections for positions on decentralized bodies, especially those at or near the local level. Those who argue this accuse parties of needlessly intensifying conflict within communities, of importing issues from higher levels which have little relevance to people at the grass roots, and so on. There is some substance in these claims, but it is unwise to seek to exclude parties—for several reasons.[14]

First, it will not work. In countries that permit competition between parties at higher levels in the system—and even when this is curtailed— party leaders will find ways round bans on their participation in local elections, by modest acts of subterfuge.[15] Since the tendency towards various types of subterfuge is unhealthy in any democratic system, it is best to avoid unenforceable bans which invite it. At first glance, we may be attracted by proposals that "community-level elections should be depoliticized through mechanisms to replace the parties with territorial neighbourhood groups and corporative organizations" (Carvajal, 1995, p. 47). But in practice, such schemes are unworkable.

We also need to recognize that the involvement of parties in local council politics yields numerous benefits. In democratic systems, it helps to integrate elected councils at the grass roots with representative structures higher up and, thereby, to deepen democracy. If conflicts of interest develop between central government and decentralized authorities, the presence of parties at all levels make them easier to manage (Gibson and Hanson, 1996).

If local councillors find that they lack the leverage to render bureaucrats responsive or accountable (because the latter have links to superiors higher up in their ministries), parties provide them with connections to elected leaders at higher levels who may be able to put things right. It assists parties in building their organizations, which by and large is a healthy thing. It enables parties to ease the discontents of ambitious people at lower levels by providing them with responsibilities and the chance to learn useful political skills. Those who perform well in local councils can then move up to higher level posts with useful experience at making democracy work. Allowing parties into local elections also creates political prizes which they can win, even if they have failed in elections higher up. This reduces the winner-take-all nature of higher level elections and eases despair and alienation among unsuccessful parties.[16] The (usually unsuccessful) attempts by autocratic regimes to ban parties from local elections—the military governments of H. M. Ershad in Bangladesh in the late 1980s and Sani Abacha in Nigeria in 1996 are examples—is eloquent testimony to the contributions which party involvement at the grass roots can make to democracy.

Finally, the presence of parties in local councils helps to promote accountability, which is crucial to the effective working of democratic decentralization. It helps, first, by organizing the opposing forces on a council into clearly recognizable groups which at subsequent elections will offer themselves to the voters for judgment. If contending forces are merely a jumble of sometimes shifting factions and alignments without labels, it is very difficult for the electorate to register a focused verdict on their record.

Second, by structuring debate and conflict on councils into a more clearly discernible pattern of ruling versus opposition groups, the presence of parties facilitates accountability between elections. It does this because opposition parties naturally seek to criticize poor performance and to unearth malfeasance—calling the ruling party to account constantly (Gazaryan and Jeleniewski, 1996, p. 62).

Popular Pressure for Decentralization

There is very little evidence to indicate that decisions by governments to decentralize were influenced by pressure from ordinary people at the grass roots (Part III). At best and occasionally, it arises from elites within certain organized interests, which is not the same thing. Three related points are worth noting.

First, would-be decentralizers should not expect concerted action from the local level in support of their plans. Rural dwellers often respond enthusiastically after decentralization occurs, but anticipatory shows of support do not—on present evidence—occur.

Second and more crucially, even when decentralized institutions take root and become popular, threats to them do not elicit grass roots protests, never mind resistance. It is common to hear enthusiasts for decentralization laugh off the jealousy of higher level politicians by saying that the masses will rise up to thwart any efforts to weaken it. They are mistaken and naive. In all of the many cases where higher-ups have eroded or destroyed decentralized authorities—some of which were quite successful and popular (for example, Crook and Manor, 1994, chapter two)—there is no evidence of preventive action at the grass roots.

Finally, it follows that the absence of such protest from below should not be taken to imply that a particular program of decentralization is unpopular. It may or may not be.

Devices to Compel Elected Representatives to Engage with People at the Grass Roots

Several experiments with decentralization have included devices to compel elected representatives in decentralized bodies to interact regularly and meaningfully with the ordinary citizens to whom they are meant to be accountable. Some readers may be surprised at the use of the words "require" and "compel" here—rather than "persuade" or "enable." But an element of compulsion is required, given the intense reluctance of most representatives to engage in any structured way (and sometimes in any way at all) with their constituents. There are some exceptions to this generalization, but they are greatly outnumbered by those which conform to it in every country for which evidence on this point is available.

Decentralizers have tried various institutional means to require representatives to engage with the citizenry. In Ghana, a novel attempt was made to require elected members of District Assemblies to perform manual labor alongside ordinary folk! But the usual approach is to demand that periodic encounters be held which tend to resemble village meetings, where constituents' views and discontents can be aired. These tend to fail (as indeed the Ghanaian provision did) because representatives either stage meetings with picked sympathizers or because they avoid any such encounter. The main problem is that the arenas within which elected representatives operate are usually so numerous and far-flung, and the monitoring capacities of central governments are so limited, that politicians find it easy to elude such encounters.

A way round this problem may have been found in Bangladesh, where a new arrangement is currently under consideration—although at this writing, it has not yet been put into practice. Instead of proposing all-inclusive meetings, the authorities are considering the creation of large committees in each local council constituency, consisting of spokespersons for a wide range of interests, including several of the more prosperous and powerful local groups. Their presence is crucial because it will make it very difficult for local councillors to avoid regular meetings with them. Enough nonelite, disadvantaged groups will also be present on these occasions to ensure that a wide array of views is heard.[17]

Some will object, rightly, that this solution is less ideal than villagewide meetings. Making the lowest level body a consultative rather than a deliberative and implementing institution curtails its powers. And since co-optation may be used to constitute part or all of such bodies, they may be less representative in an electoral sense—though co-optation, when properly handled, can enhance representativeness. Representatives of poor and excluded groups (including women) will have more clout if they are elected rather than co-opted. And since such bodies are likely to be less formally institutionalized than elected councils higher up, there may be a tendency not to empower them as much as those higher level councils. But given the minimal implementation capacity at the lowest levels in all political systems, little will probably be lost as a result. And, crucially, since such encounters are more likely to take place than villagewide meetings, this approach is well worth trying. (There may be similar arrangements elsewhere, particularly in some Latin American countries, but the available information from there is currently fragmentary and unclear.)

Utility of Participatory Rural Appraisal Techniques

There is another way to tackle the problems assessed in the previous section. Governments which are genuinely interested in reinforcing and integrating the increased responsiveness of government institutions, and the enhanced participation and associational activity within society which usually result from democratic decentralization, are well advised to consider using participatory rural appraisal techniques.

These techniques are not infallible and should not be overestimated or oversold. But, as readers of the literature on participatory rural appraisal have seen, they can help to identify what rural dwellers perceive as their most urgent problems and what they prefer as solutions—thus drawing on local knowledge and often well-tested, informal local solutions to them. (For evidence on the urgency of this, see Leach and Mearns, 1996.) They can assist in monitoring efforts to solve problems and in identifying deserving beneficiaries among the poor.

Certain other advantages which participatory rural appraisal techniques offer may, however, be less familiar. Like democratic decentralization, they tend to catalyze increased participation and associational activity at the grass roots. And when used by or in conjunction with decentralized authorities, they can help to knit the responsiveness of those institutions together more intimately with the quickening participation and associational activity that those authorities inspire. They can heighten popular awareness of local problems and potential solutions among rural dwellers. When this happens in one locality, neighbouring communities tend to hear of it and seek to follow suit (Gaventa, 1997).[18]

The use of participatory rural appraisal techniques can also heighten the appetites and demands of ordinary people at the local level for greater participation and consultation. This intensifies pressure on decentralized authorities to be accountable to ordinary folk—a matter of crucial importance. It can facilitate accountability, but such demands also promote conflict both with local elites (sometimes including elected members of local authorities) and with power holders at higher levels in political systems. A certain amount of such conflict is inevitable and healthy, since it helps to promote social justice and more effective partnerships between state and society. But it can also create problems. This kind of politics is not necessarily a zero-sum game (Arnstein, 1969 and Gaventa, 1997). Such conflict can cause influential people to lose some of their enthusiasm for democratic decentralization and, in extremis, place its survival in jeopardy.

Notes

1. See, on Latin America, Nickson (1995, p. 3). I am grateful to Jean-François Bayart for calling my attention to similar tendencies in the literature on francophone Africa.

2. Since we are discussing democratic decentralization, popular participation—which might also be seen as crucial—is assumed to be present. Participation alone does not guarantee the success of experiments with decentralization (Crook and Manor, 1994).

3. I am grateful to Jorge Dominguez for this insight and form of words.

4. Interview with B. Rachiah, Bangalore, January 11, 1988.

5. Times of India, March 15, 1996.

6. See for example World Bank (1995, p. ix) and much of the literature on decentralization in Bangladesh, which is dominated by public administration specialists.

7. I am grateful to T. Mathew of the Indian Administrative Service for information on this.

8. See the studies of Estonia, Poland, Hungary and the Czech Republic, and the conclusion of Gibson and Hanson (1996), and the European Bank for Reconstruction and Development (EBRD) (1994).

9. Discussion with Harry Blair, London, April 17, 1997.

10. I am grateful to V.K. Natraj for calling this to my attention. There are suggestions of this in de los Reyes and Jopillo, 1995.

11. Interview with a civil servant who was present on that occasion, Brighton, March 17, 1997.

12. John Gaventa has evidence of such trends even within the United States.

13. The words here are not Hirschman's but are from a summary of his studies in Haggard and Kaufman, 1992.

14. See for example, Robinson (1988).

15. This was true in Bangladesh under H.M. Ershad's military regime between 1985 and 1991.

16. The utility of this for democracy, civil society and policymakers is vividly apparent from Jenkins, (1997) on the Indian state of Maharashtra.

17. I am grateful to Bangladeshi colleagues at a workshop on decentralization at Rajendrapur, March 10–11, 1997, for calling this to my attention.

18. For example, John Gaventa found clear evidence of this in the Philippines in 1997.

Part V
Assessing Desentralization to the Regional as well as the Local Level

Q uestions from some policy specialists suggest that it is worth considering the advantages and disadvantages that attend decentralization to a level between the national and the local levels—the regional or intermediate level—as well as the local level. This is important partly because decentralization to both levels is extremely common, and partly because it tends to offer greater promise than decentralization to only one of those levels.

This analysis is inevitably somewhat crude and abstract. The degree and character of regional variations differ greatly from country to country. Power and resources have been decentralized to different regional levels (some high and some low) in different countries. But most of the comments below are true in most circumstances. (There is, unavoidably, a certain amount of repetition here of points from Part VI.)

The Greater Complexity and Cost of Decentralization to Both Regional and Local Levels

Decentralization to both regional and local levels is more complicated than to the local level alone. More things can go wrong as a result. It is also more expensive. There are, however, countervailing advantages (as all of the other sections in Part V indicate).

Bridging the Distance between Central and Local Levels

A huge conceptual and actual distance separates central governments and the grass roots in all but the smallest countries. If only local-level authorities are created, it is often well-nigh impossible for elected members to comprehend, communicate with, or influence central governments and the upper reaches of their administrative agencies. The simultaneous creation of regional-level authorities provides a crucially important mechanism to integrate local and central levels, as several of the points which follow illustrate.

Which Responsibilities Should be Decentralized to Which Levels?

It is widely understood that it makes sense to decentralize those responsibilities in which economies of scale cannot be achieved. We also note below that it is unwise to devolve responsibility for complex development projects onto local-level authorities because they tend to lack the inclination, the sophistication and the administrative capacity to implement them. It also makes sense to avoid devolving the control of projects which extend spatially beyond a single local arena onto authorities in such arenas.

But responsibility for many complex programs and for projects extending over more than one locality can usefully be devolved onto *regional-level* authorities. This will enhance the chances of integrating local preferences, local knowledge of particularistic needs, and the often quite creative local methods and mechanisms for managing resources, resolving conflicts, and the like, into the official decisionmaking process.

Local representatives can often play extremely creative roles in facilitating the implementation even of technically complicated national programs. For example, elected members of local and sometimes regional authorities can explain to villagers the utility of national inoculation programs—and because villagers trust them, this can increase the uptake on such services. The existence of regional-level authorities can facilitate such things.

Protecting Decentralization from the Jealousy of Higher Level Leaders

When decentralization occurs not just to the local level, but to the regional level too, it gives decentralized institutions a better chance to resist attempts by national-level politicians and bureaucrats to take back powers and resources devolved onto them. High-level leaders often do this because they feel weakened by decentralization (even though it strengthens them in many ways). Regional-level institutions have much more leverage in national politics than do local-level institutions.

Decentralizers should be aware that politicians at the regional level often experience the same pangs of jealousy towards local-level authorities as central leaders do towards all authorities at lower levels (World Bank, 1997a; Crook and Manor, 1994). They therefore need to ensure that local authorities are adequately empowered, lest centralizers at the regional level undermine them. But in most systems, this problem appears to have been minimized.

Enhancing the Influence of Decentralized Bodies in National Politics

For the same reason, regional-level institutions are better able to represent the interests of the decentralized system in national politics than local institutions alone—even where national politicians do not try to claw back power.

Ensuring Poor, Remote Regions of Fairer Representation in National Politics

Decentralization to the regional level usually gives (often poor, remote) regions which have lacked adequate representation in national politics a chance to exert greater influence than before. It also gives under-resourced regions a better chance to gain a fairer share of resources. These things are much more difficult if only local-level institutions are created.

Facilitating Local Authorities' Access to Administrative Resources at the Regional Level

Regional institutions can assist local institutions with a chronic problem—administrative incapacity. Local institutions may only have one or two poorly trained bureaucrats, but regional-level bodies usually have sizeable administrative staffs. It is easier for locals to draw on regional staffs if elected politicians enjoy some influence at the regional level.

The best way to ensure that they have such influence is to have members of regional-level authorities elected by local-level councils. However, this form of indirect election has two disadvantages. It deprives such politicians of a strong electoral mandate directly from voters. And it makes regional authorities only indirectly accountable to voters. As a result, direct election of members of regional authorities is probably preferable, but both systems can work reasonably well.

Enhancing Coordination of Development Administrators from Different Line Ministries.

Regional institutions can and often do achieve impressive results at coordinating administrative staff from different line ministries. This is almost impossible if only local-level institutions exist.

Facilitating Complex Development Projects

Regional institutions are much more able and willing to manage somewhat complex development projects. Local institutions tend to undertake only very simple projects. Many of these are valuable, but more complex projects are also necessary.

Facilitating Scaling Up from the Local Level

Regional institutions make it much easier to scale up from the local level. If only local institutions exist, it is much harder to ensure that successful experiments in isolated localities are replicated elsewhere.

Facilitating the Upward Flow of Information from the Local Level and the Responsiveness of Central Government

Regional institutions make it much easier to ensure that information from below is fed effectively into the national administrative system, and that responses are made to local-level needs. If only local institutions exist, this is very difficult.

Combating Absenteeism and Irresponsible Behaviour by Government Employees

In some decentralized systems, pressure has been brought to bear by decentralized institutions on government employees (in, for example, schools and health clinics) who do not turn up for work or who behave irresponsibly in other ways. This is much more difficult if only local institutions exist, because they often lack the leverage which regional institutions possess over such employees.

Enhancing the Accountability and Responsiveness of Regional-Level Bureaucrats

Regional institutions are also much more able than local bodies to apply pressure to intermediate-level bureaucrats, to make them accountable, and to prevent them from responding only to their national-level superiors in line ministries.

Facilitating Poverty Alleviation and Fairness for Minorities.

In many countries, elite prejudices against poor groups and minorities are stronger at the local level than at the national level. When this is true, such prejudices at the regional level tend to be less strong than at the grass roots. In such circumstances, decentralization to the regional as well as the local level can help prevent decentralization from damaging the interests of the poor or minorities.

Facilitating Fairness to Women

Prejudices against women are also stronger in many countries at the local level than at higher levels. Regional institutions therefore often give women representatives a greater chance to achieve things, and ensure greater attention to the needs of female citizens.

Easing the Problem of the Foreshortened Time Perspective of Local-Level Politicians

People who gain power in local-level institutions often have a more foreshortened time perspective than those at higher levels—and this affects their development plans. If regional institutions are created, they can often ease this problem.

Facilitating Collaboration between Nongovernmental Organizations and Decentralized Authorities

Indigenous nongovernmental organizations often find it easier to collaborate with decentralized institutions when they exist at both regional and local levels rather than just the local level. This tends to be true both because attitudes in regional institutions are sometimes more enlightened than at the grass roots, and because regional institutions have much more administrative capacity.

Integrating the Efforts of Local-Level Voluntary Associations

Decentralization often causes political participation and the activity and the number of voluntary associations to increase. It is much easier to integrate such activities in different localities—and to strengthen democracy—if decentralized institutions exist not just at the local level but at the regional level too.

Overcoming Authoritarian Enclaves

Democratic decentralization can help to overcome authoritarian enclaves in political systems making the transition to democracy. This is one reason that the South African government has introduced it into the former "bantustans" where hereditary chiefs dominated politics. But it is also a concern in places such as the Philippines, Thailand and parts of Latin America where "local (or regional) bossism" is a problem (Sidel, 1997; and Fox, 1994). It is far easier to achieve this (and to consolidate democracy) if democratic decentralization occurs not just to the local level, but to the regional level too.

Facilitating the Integration of Local-Level Politicians into National Politics

One advantage of decentralization is that it gives aspiring politicians many more openings into the political system. It therefore becomes a training ground for democracy, and it eases the sometimes dangerous frustration of people excluded from political careers. If regional institutions exist, then successful politicians at the local level find it easier to gain promotion to higher levels. Their entry into national politics therefore becomes easier, and the promise that democracy offers will seem to them (and, indeed, will be) greater.

Facilitating the Integration of Competing Political Parties into Decentralized Institutions

If regional as well as local institutions exist, they facilitate the integration of political parties into decentralized systems. Some people believe that political parties should not play a role in these systems. But it is almost impossible to keep them out, and the evidence suggests that party competition in decentralized systems can make them healthier and more transparent.

Combating Urban Bias

Regional institutions can also help to combat urban bias in government development policies, providing that representatives from an urban center do not dominate the regional institution. (For more detail on this, see below.)

Part VI
How Promising is Decentralization for Rural Development?

How much promise does decentralization offer for efforts to promote rural development? To answer this question, we need to consider a long list of problems that have beset rural development strategies. Some repetition of points from Parts IV and V is inevitable here.

This discussion is divided into three sections. The first section deals with matters in which decentralization—*on currently available empirical evidence, and in the near future*—has considerable promise. The second section addresses matters in which it has more limited promise, and the third section notes areas in which it has little promise.

In considering what follows, readers need to remember two things. First, there is a distinct shortage of reliable evidence about the workings of many (though not all) experiments with decentralization. Second, we are assessing institutions that are still quite young. Only a few originated before 1985, and some of them were abandoned or markedly changed after only a short time. Some of the most adventurous experiments—for example, Bolivia's—have only just got underway.

If these exercises are allowed to continue for sustained periods—a big if, given higher level politicians' jealousy of decentralized institutions—their performance on several of the fronts listed below will probably improve. There are signs, in many different countries, that this has begun to happen. So in time, some of the items listed in sections B and C are quite likely to move up to level A or B. The analysis below should be seen not as the final word on this subject, but as an assessment of how things look now—at what is probably an unfairly early stage in the life spans of most of these experiments. So as we noted at the outset, even where the judgments offered below appear to be forceful assertions, they should be read as provisional assessments which may very well change over time.

Where Decentralization Has Considerable Promise

Decentralization has promise for many key objectives. The main ones are described below.

Reversing the neglect of institutional development

It has been noted that when central governments created high-level coordination units, they undermined the development of institutional capacity at lower levels to foster and execute rural development (World Bank, 1987). The devolution of powers and resources to lower levels will itself enhance capacity at those levels. And empowerment will enable influential people at those levels to press for further enhancement of institutional capacity to perform these tasks. (This is not to say, however, that decentralized bodies will necessarily become effective at every developmental task. Planning, for example, is a difficult area.)

Promoting greater participation and associational activity

Evidence from South Asia and West Africa clearly indicates that substantial (though often less-than-spectacular) gains can be made here through democratic decentralization (Crook and Manor, 1994). Participation grows both at elections (in terms of voting and of participating in campaigns) and between them—through increased contact or petitioning of elected representatives and (to a lesser degree) of bureaucrats, through attending official and unofficial meetings, through protests, and the like. It should be noted that poorer, low status groups tend strongly to exercise less influence and to receive fewer benefits than more prosperous groups in such cases. But participation by and associational activity within all groups tends to increase significantly.

This tends to occur even where civil society (organized interests) has previously been weak. We saw in section II that for democratic decentralization to work reasonably well, it was not essential to have either a lively civil society or an abundance of social capital, but that both things are helpful. Since democratic decentralization fosters both of those things, sustained experiments with it can be expected, over time, to gain strength from both of these things (see, however, "Community Participation in Development," below).

We should understand, however, that increased participation can also pose a threat. When it occurs, expectations and demands tend to rise. If decentralized bodies distribute benefits mainly among elites or malfunction in other ways, the result can be widespread anger. The same thing can happen if high-level authorities undermine decentralized bodies. Popular anger is not always a bad thing, but it is not what decentralizers intend.

Enhancing the responsiveness of government institutions

One crucial caveat is in order here. Where decentralization is democratic in character, responsiveness nearly always improves markedly. But administrative or fiscal decentralization which is unattended by democratization holds little promise here—despite naive comments to the contrary, unsupported by evidence, here and there in the literature.

Democratic decentralization tends strongly to enhance the *speed, quantity and quality* of responses from government institutions. Since it usually entails some empowerment and autonomy for elected bodies at intermediate or local levels, or both, those bodies usually possess the authority and resources to respond quickly to problems and pressures from below— without waiting for the approval of agencies at higher levels. The evidence from a wide array of cases indicates that this quickens responses.

Since decentralized bodies have a strong bias towards microlevel infrastructure projects, and since such projects are less costly than large-scale programs often preferred by central authorities, the quantity of outputs from government also tends to increase markedly.

Since democratic decentralization provides interests at the grass roots with influence over decisions within bodies at intermediate or local levels, the quality of such outputs is also usually enhanced—if quality is measured by the degree to which such outputs conform to the preferences of ordinary people.

Solid evidence of gains is available from an extremely broad array of countries and cultures. Opinion surveys in Colombia indicated very high levels of enthusiasm for the spending priorities of municipios. This was true even though different *municipios* emphasized different sectors (water here, roads there)—the explanation being that local needs and preferences differed from place to place. Similarly high levels of general satisfaction with the performance of these institutions were also expressed (World Bank, 1995, pp. 5–6).

Evidence corroborating such trends emerges from, among others, the Philippines, India, Bangladesh, Sri Lanka and Côte d'Ivoire (Panganiban, 1994; de los Reyes and Jopillo, 1995; Crook and Manor, 1994).[1] (These findings contradict the misinformed assertion in the *World Development Report 1997* that "little comparative evidence is available with which to evaluate the relationship between decentralized government and service quality" (World Bank, 1997a, p. 123).

Increasing the information flow between government and people

This is again quite commonly a major gain from democratic decentralization. Elected members and heads of local and/or intermediate authorities usually live near or within their constituencies (unlike many members of higher level parliaments). Voters know that these people owe their position to a popular mandate and that they (usually) have the power to shape government action, so they tend to put their views to these representatives and to bureaucrats more often than before decentralization.

This results in a considerable, and often a huge increase in the amount of information flowing to persons in government—especially, but not only, where there is a lively civil society. District-level bureaucrats in the Indian state of Karnataka, for example, repeatedly stated that they experienced something like a tenfold increase in information after decentralization there. Before it occurred, they had thought that they had an abundance of information—from their own administrative networks, state legislators, the free press, and the like—but thereafter they realized that they had been woefully underinformed. They felt empowered by the change and experienced a surge in job satisfaction (Crook and Manor, 1994).

Democratic decentralization also, although to a somewhat lesser degree, enhances the flow of information from government to citizens. This is partly the result of the (nearly always substantial, and sometimes massive) increase in the number of elected representatives who act as conduits for information from the bureaucracy and elected bodies to people at the grass roots. It also owes much to the ability of those representatives to break down popular suspicion of government by explaining official projects in terms that are intelligible to ordinary people. Major gains often occur, for example, in government programs for preventive medicine—vaccination campaigns, efforts to screen rural dwellers for serious diseases which need to be caught early, prenatal and postnatal care, and others—but not only these (Manor, 1995).[2]

Providing early warnings of potential disasters

One immensely beneficial example of improved information flows to government is the provision of early warnings of problems which, if left unattended, can burgeon into disasters—especially droughts, public sanitation problems and outbreaks of disease. Prior to decentralization, when signs of these things emerge—especially but not just in remote and under-represented areas—warnings often fail to reach the appropriate authorities soon enough to make action possible. After decentralization—which tends both to provide better representation for remote, underdeveloped areas and to give representatives from those areas the leverage to animate government agencies—early warnings and official responses occur far more often and reliably.

Major gains on this front were reported even from a region of India which had long had democratic representation (albeit only in state and national legislatures), a lively civil society, and a free press given to investigative doings (Crook and Manor, 1994). In places where such things have traditionally been absent, the gains can be expected to be proportionally greater.

Making development projects more sustainable

It is widely recognized in the literature that if people at the grass roots are drawn, even quite marginally, into decisions or just discussions about rural development projects, they develop the belief that they have a stake in their success. And since the quality of responses from government institutions tends to improve in the sense that they are more congruent with locally felt needs, people naturally identify more strongly with development projects.

This does a great deal to make those projects more sustainable. This applies to the management of natural resources, service delivery and much else. See for example a United Nations Development Programme—World Bank study of 121 rural water supply projects (Parker, 1995, p. 44; and Narayan, 1994).

Enhancing transparency

Democratic decentralization holds great promise here. When large numbers of decentralized bodies are thrown open to people who usually live within their constituencies, their neighbours and constituents become far better able to see and understand what goes on within government institutions. The same is true of the elected representatives themselves, who explain their doings and decisions in order to cultivate popular support (Crook and Manor, 1994; de los Reyes and Jopillo, 1995). When multiparty competition occurs within these systems, as it usually does, opposition forces constantly raise questions about the conduct of those in the majority and publicize news (or allegations) of misdeeds. These changes bring to an end the era when something as basic as the amount of funds available for development was known only to a handful of people high up in the system (a situation that facilitated large-scale, clandestine thefts of funds). Politics and the development process tend to become more untidy and contentious, but also more open and intelligible than before.

Promoting greater accountability

For all of the reasons set out just above, and because positions of power are obtained by election, democratic decentralization tends to enhance the accountability of elected representatives to citizens. This does not guarantee that elected leaders will be models of probity, responsiveness or efficiency. But if they fail badly in these respects, voters tend to oust them at the first opportunity. Once that has happened to one or two sets of leaders, citizens acquire a taste for rejecting poor representatives, and their successors in office grasp the meaning of accountability, so that it becomes likely that their conduct will improve over time.

It is more difficult to ensure the other, equally crucial type of accountability—of bureaucrats to elected representatives. That can only be achieved if high-level decentralizers empower lower level authorities to exercise influence over bureaucrats, and then back them with helpful interventions where necessary. Those are two big ifs, but this sort of thing has happened often enough to warrant cautious optimism here.

Exercising regulatory functions

We note below that decentralized authorities sometimes have difficulty with monitoring, evaluation and planning from below. But the fragmentary evidence which is available suggests that they can be quite effective and—crucially, more responsive to local sentiments—at carrying out small-scale regulatory functions. In the Philippines, such bodies exercised great care over land use issues. They did well "in managing the establishment of cockpits and holding of cockfights, regulating the operation of tricycles for hire, inspection of food products, enforcement of the National Building Code, and legislation and enforcement of environment-related laws" (de los Reyes and Jopillo, p. 81). Cockfights may be a rather specialized interest, but several of these other roles are of considerable importance. (See also, Crook and Manor, 1994.)

Achieving political renewal

The creation of elected authorities at intermediate and local levels opens up a large number of positions of power for people—many of them young—who aspire to political influence. This eases the frustration of such people and deflects them from destructive behaviour which often results from exasperation with limited opportunities. (This can develop even in long-established democracies. In the Indian state of Karnataka, there were 224 elected posts in the legislature before decentralization in 1987, and afterward there were more than 50,000! For corroborating evidence from the Philippines, see de los Reyes and Jopillo, 1995, p. 79.)

When leaders of voluntary associations and other organized interests near the local level seize these opportunities, as they routinely do, it integrates state and society in potentially creative ways. These people develop the skills and attitudes that are needed to make the politics of bargaining and accommodation work. The ensuing gains tend to outweigh the problems (such as elite capture of decentralized authorities) which often attend such changes. This can also greatly facilitate institutional capacity building (World Bank, 1995, p. viii; Manor, 1995).

Reinforcing national-level democracy

This process is closely tied to the item just above, but it is slightly different. Jonathan Fox has ably shown that democratic decentralization to intermediate and local levels strengthens democracy at the national level. This is true in both new and old democracies, although Fox is mainly concerned with recently democratized systems in Latin America. It does so in four interrelated ways:

> First, elected civilian regimes cannot be considered democratic until authoritarian enclaves are eliminated and the entire citizenry is effectively enfranchised. Second, pluralist politics must be learned, and subnational governments make a good school. Third, rising democratic leaders can most credibly challenge the corrupt old ways if they are forearmed with successful records in local government. Fourth, the widespread transition from traditionally paternalistic social policies to more efficient and targeted programs depends on balanced partnerships among national governments, and new social and civil actors (Fox, 1994, p. 106).

Where Decentralization Has at Least Modest Promise

Evidence suggests that decentralization has some promise for a number of objectives. These are described below.

Broadening the overly narrow focus on agricultural productivity

The record of elected authorities in Africa and Asia onto which power
has been devolved shows a consistent tendency to direct resources into
activities of public benefit which have little connection with agricultural productivity. That is good news for those who complain that
some rural development programs are too narrowly preoccupied with
productivity.

There is, however, bad news here too. These authorities tend to
focus, again narrowly, on small-scale construction projects—road
repairs, bridges, school rooms, and wells. This often (but not always)
means that the delivery of important services—education, health, agricultural extension, animal husbandry, and the like—suffer at least a little. (But note that in Latin America, there appears to be more interest
in service delivery.)[3] So on this front, decentralization can be a mixed
blessing.

Some governments have eased this problem by earmarking portions
of grants to decentralized authorities for important services and sectors, while giving those authorities influence over specific decisions
within those sectors (Crook and Manor, 1994, chapters two and three).
But it is often difficult to know and to ensure that large number of
decentralized bodies are adhering to the rules governing earmarking.

Making development programs more flexible so that they suit local conditions

Where decentralization is substantially democratic, local interests often
succeed in persuading elected politicians to allocate funds to those elements of programs which best suit local needs—thus rendering them
less inflexible (Ruttan, 1984). We can also include here initiatives to
ease the problem of lack of appropriate technology (World Bank, 1987).
Local interests tend to press for adaptations in technology and project
design to meet their particular needs. If projects cannot be adapted in
this way, they often refuse to approve or implement them—which is,
on balance, also good news.

Decentralized authorities also tend to excel (when, crucially, they are
empowered to do so) at adapting nationally designed laws and tax
codes to local peculiarities, minimizing irrelevant matters and perni-
cious mandates in ways that harmonize with local conditions. This
can, among others, enhance revenues from local property taxes. In the
Philippines, this has been the "most remarkable strength" of local
authorities (de los Reyes and Jopillo, 1995, p. 88).

There is, however, bad news here too. Elected representatives—especially those standing near the village level—often find it difficult to understand any technologically complex proposal. They therefore tend to direct resources away from all such initiatives, and to favor comparatively simple construction projects as noted just above. This often means that technologies do not get adapted to local conditions.

Changing adverse policy environments for agriculture

When this problem thwarted integrated rural development programs in the 1980s, the adverse policy environment existed at the national level (World Bank, 1987). Decentralization empowers arenas where agriculture is of greater concern, but it also brings with it a strong bias in favor of microlevel construction projects, some of which do not serve the needs of farmers. In other words, the policy environment at lower levels is often only somewhat less adverse.

Reinforcing central government commitment to rural development

This relates closely to the previous section (World Bank, 1987). Decentralization offers certain potential gains here, since rural development will count for more among rural dwellers to whom power is devolved. But three things need to be set against that.

First, as noted just above, many projects implemented by local authorities do little to assist agriculturists. Second, the small infrastructure projects which those authorities prefer often fail to conform to the central government views of what constitutes rural development, and that can create conflicts which may undermine higher level leaders' commitments to such development. Finally, those leaders higher up are notoriously jealous of the powers and resources given to those at lower levels. This may tend to erode central commitment to authorities lower down and, in the process, to reinforce central prejudices against rural development.

Giving greater attention to sociocultural factors

When groups at lower levels have influence, they tend strongly to ensure that programs which fly in the face of regional or local customs, preferences or social structures are either adapted or rejected—sometimes clandestinely in both cases. This, again, has mixed implications.

It means that resources are not wasted on inappropriate initiatives—a major gain. Decentralization can also help to resolve collective action problems in the management of common property resources by incorporating into the formal political process local knowledge and informal local arrangements for coping with these problems—although this sometimes excludes pastoralists, to their disadvantage (Bardhan, 1997, Leach and Mearns, 1996). But it can also mean that groups which suffer discrimination as a result of local biases (hierarchical mentalities, or prejudice against minorities) are denied benefits.

Mitigating the damaging effects of "hegemonic Western modernity"

This theme is often stressed both by postmodernists and by analysts who are concerned about the damage which intrusions from on high can do to the way of life of grass roots communities. (Those two groups overlap somewhat). Many development specialists prefer to ignore or to dismiss their views. But some of these writers are acutely perceptive and deserve to be taken seriously, especially those who do not idealize local communities and exaggerate the harmony therein (Kothari, 1988 and 1989; and Nandy, 1988).

These writers tend to favor decentralization as a way of providing people at the local level with at least some means of defending themselves from unwelcome aspects of development fueled either by the centralized state or by potent market forces. Both of these are seen as aggregations of power that can do severe damage by treating cherished local beliefs, moral codes, informal processes for managing local affairs, and valuable local diversities—many of which are far from antidevelopment—dismissively and aggressively.

Decentralization provides only limited resources to local communities in this struggle. But insofar as it renders government institutions more responsive, and enables local-level interests to undertake small-scale projects of their own choosing—as it commonly does—it has considerable value. There is no reason why we should exclude these concerns from our definition of rural development.

This is not to say that decentralized institutions find it easy to mesh with voluntary associations at and near the local level. Their relations are problematic even in the best of circumstances (Crook and Manor, 1994). But there are modest benefits to be had which should not be ignored in this discussion.

Those in central governments who fear that their own programs and perspectives will be overwhelmed by local prejudices as a result of decentralization are worrying needlessly. The evidence clearly indicates that they retain much of their former potency, and that the real danger is that local preferences will be given too few opportunities to influence decisions. There are also ways to ensure that central programs and policies remain highly influential, while drawing local interests into creative partnerships.

Assisting ethnic or religious minorities

This item is closely tied to the preceding section. When ethnic or religious minorities are concentrated in particular subregions or localities, then the devolution of power onto arenas which are roughly congruent with them can enable such groups to gain greater control of their destiny, and to defend themselves against unwanted intrusions from above (Dukesbury, 1991). This can ease their alienation from the state and the wider society, and reduce the danger of damaging conflict.

But the precise details of political geography are crucial here. Such minorities often live cheek by jowl with majority groups, and when that is true, decentralization may actually empower arenas in which prejudices against minorities are stronger than at higher levels in the political system. It may make things worse. Architects of decentralization need to consider this possibility when framing their plans.

Assisting women

The limited evidence available on the impact of decentralization on women's interests offers only modest encouragement. It appears that the empowerment of arenas at or near the local level, where prejudices against women are often stronger than at higher levels, may damage their prospects unless provisions are made to give women a meaningful voice. In some systems, some seats on councils are reserved for women nominees. This holds little promise for them, because they tend to be beholden to the male leaders who secured their nomination. Their best hope lies in the reservation of seats for which only women candidates can stand for election, but this appears to have been attempted in only a few places—notably India.

Even there, it has so far yielded only minimal benefits. During the five-year life span of one such system there, in which 25 percent of seats were so reserved, women members of intermediate-level councils combined to act in women's interests only very exceptionally—less often than ex-untouchable members did. (Some women councillors managed to break down suspicions of village women about health and child welfare programs, however, so that participation in them improved in certain areas.) In local-level councils there, no evidence whatsoever of such action was uncovered by an extensive search for it. By the end of the five years, there were indications that more formidable, educated women would come forward at the next election at the intermediate level (Crook and Manor, 1994, chapter two). But gains for women remain more a hope than a reality.

Facilitating scaling up from successful pilot projects

If projects are shaped very substantially by a desire to suit local particularities—as frequently occurs within elected authorities near the local level—this can create some difficulties in scaling up, in making successful pilot projects more widely applicable. But in most countries, variations in conditions from one locality to another are not so radical as to render successful pilot projects nonreplicable. Far more tends to be gained as a result of consultations with and support from local interests than is lost in replicability.

Combating the tendency to sacrifice local needs to the administrative convenience of generalizers

To reiterate the obvious: the empowerment of elected bodies at or near the local level tends strongly to give interests at the grass roots considerable influence over the shape of development projects. They are unlikely to permit the imposition of initiatives crafted by generalizers at higher levels which fly in the face of local particularities and felt needs.

Politicians and bureaucrats at higher levels should be encouraged to recognize that this presents them not just with a problem, but also with an opportunity. If they develop dialogues with decentralized bodies on macrolevel programs, they will find that partnerships with these authorities can facilitate public understanding of, participation in, and support for those programs—most impressively in mass inoculation and other initiatives in preventive medicine, public health and sanitation, but not only these.

Such partnerships serve the interests of everyone, including high-level power holders. This offers some compensation for the erosion both of their formerly complete control over such programs and of their commandist powers more generally, although it is exceedingly difficult to persuade them of this.

Tackling the problem of complexity and coordination

This is an area in which decentralization offers promise and poses potentially serious difficulties. It is promising in two rather different ways. First, as Binswanger (1994) has noted, coordination issues at lower levels in political systems are usually less complex than at higher levels, and institutions at lower levels often have the incentives, the ability and—especially—the information to achieve positive results.

Second, when authorities at lower levels possess wide-ranging powers over rural development programs, it is easier for them to bring the employees of several line ministries together for consultation and concerted action than is possible at higher levels. For example, in the late 1980s in both Bangladesh and the Indian state of Karnataka, elected leaders found it possible to draw together, frequently, officials from a broad range of government departments to discuss development projects. As a result, when a proposal to develop a small-scale irrigation scheme was considered, advice was regularly available not just from irrigation specialists, but from engineers and officials dealing with agriculture, fisheries and other activities affected by and affecting the scheme. They discussed the project not just with one another but with representatives of the local communities that would be affected by it, and the resulting synergy yielded significant benefits. It would have been impossible to achieve this if the consultation had occurred in the capital cities of Bangladesh or Karnataka, where line ministries interact far less often (Crook and Manor, 1994).

On the other hand, Parker (1995, pp. 16-17) is not mistaken when he describes coordination as "the Achilles heel of rural development." The problem is that key leaders at lower levels sometimes lack the sophistication or the authority, or both, to succeed at coordination.

Even though, as Parker says, the small-scale projects which arise in rural development programs are "dramatically simpler" than huge projects like major irrigation systems, the people who might coordinate such projects (elected representatives and bureaucrats) may lack the training, confidence and social skills needed to succeed.

Even if they possess these things, they may not have the power to insist that officials from various line ministries shed their time-honored reluctance to collaborate. Or, as Parker notes, implementation of such projects may be delegated to "government bureaucracies or parastatals that were typically highly centralized...(and) out of touch with beneficiaries" (Parker, 1995). Elected office holders or presiding generalist bureaucrats may not have the authority to compel specialists in line ministries or parastatals to work cooperatively with specialists in other fields (Gesellschaft für Technische Zusammenarbeit, 1993).

So decentralization poses both opportunities and dangers for greater coordination. It also needs to be recognized that decentralized authorities—especially those at or near the grass roots—tend to pursue a narrower range of projects than integrated rural development programs have advocated (although those programs may have been unrealistically broad).

Maintaining complex, integrated rural development programs

As noted just above, it is unrealistic to expect decentralized authorities to tackle the full array of projects which integrated rural development programs have advocated. Many such projects will be undertaken, but the bias will be toward microlevel building projects, sometimes at the expense of service delivery. In India and Bangladesh, this problem was minimized when higher level authorities earmarked proportions of funds devolved onto local councils for various types of undertakings, with elected councils being given limited latitude for movement of funds from one budget heading to another. That did not solve the problem, but it may offer the best middle way in the drive to achieve integrated development.

Promoting cooperation between nongovernmental organizations and government

The limited evidence available indicates that democratic decentralization can make only a very limited contribution on this front, although it is possible that over time, more significant gains may emerge. International nongovernmental organizations which become frustrated with the inadequacies of central governments have sometimes found it more productive to work through decentralized authorities. But the more important issue here is the relationship between such authorities and indigenous nongovernmental organizations which are active at intermediate or local levels, or both.

We have seen that democratic decentralization can draw leaders of organized interests at the grass roots into creative roles on and relationships with decentralized bodies. But this should not be taken to imply that great progress has been made in breaking down the strong suspicions which many indigenous nongovernmental organizations harbor toward all government institutions. The limited evidence that is available even from relatively successful experiments with decentralization indicates that nongovernmental organizations seldom develop more than a tentative, cautious, arms-length relationship with these bodies, and that they are nearly as distrustful of elected leaders in such institutions as they are of power holders at higher levels. This problem may diminish over time as decentralization breaks down suspicions of government.

This writer's interviews in South Asia both with elected members of decentralized authorities and with high-level enthusiasts for decentralization have uncovered significant suspicions in both groups of indigenous nongovernmental organizations. Nongovernmental organizations are often seen as unelected, insufficiently accountable and somewhat unrepresentative. Government is seen as the main and largely sufficient engine for rural development.[4] Breaking down the suspicions on both sides of this divide will take time and may never occur in many places. We lack and badly need evidence on the workings of those few systems which give indigenous nongovernmental organizations representation within state-sponsored bodies—often of a consultative type.

Reducing absenteeism among government employees

In a very small number of cases—mainly the Indian state of Karnataka between 1987 and 1991 (Crook and Manor, 1994) and to a limited extent, the Philippines[5]—the empowerment of elected councils near the local level has enabled popular representatives to put pressure on government employees in schools and local health centers to come to work in accordance with their contracts, and to work assiduously while they are on the job. The existence of a lively civil society in these places was also crucial since it meant that citizens brought poor performance to the attention of elected representatives. This ensured that services were delivered more effectively, at no additional cost to the exchequer.

In most places, however, this needs to be seen as a possibility (once democratic decentralization has had time to establish itself) rather than as a likely gain. But if decentralized institutions are given time to take root, and if organized interests grow accustomed to engaging with them, there is some hope of headway on this front.

Reducing the overall amount of corruption

It should be stressed that democratic decentralization is always attended by an increase in the number of persons who are involved in corrupt acts. This is inevitable because it increases (usually dramatically) the number of people with at least minimal access to political power. However, this need not imply that the overall amount of money diverted by corrupt means increases. Decentralization can, in some circumstances, cause it to decline.

We have seen signs of this in a very small number of cases, especially in the Indian state of Karnataka. It also appears to have occurred in the Indian state of West Bengal—although this owes much to the presence of a penetrative and reasonably disciplined Communist Party, a factor which is seldom on hand elsewhere. It may have occurred in certain pockets in the Philippines.[6]

The crucial question here—to which we have no satisfactory answer—is: what caused this decline? Is it explained by factors external to the decentralized system, or by the system itself? Both clearly played a role, but which was crucial? If unusual externalities largely explain it, then it may be difficult to replicate this effect in other decentralized systems.

In Karnataka, the existence of a lively civil society, a large number of experienced if small-time political activists at low levels in the system, an established two-party system, a free press—external factors—helped to reduce corruption. These things are seldom found in abundance in other developing countries. But democratic decentralization provided the mechanisms through which they could produce this effect.

The available evidence strongly suggests that this is exceedingly difficult to achieve. We know of no examples other than the three mentioned above. But if strong, democratic, decentralized institutions are allowed to function for extended periods (a decade or more)—something on which we have next to no evidence—corruption might well be reduced. This might occur through a combination of processes: with democratic institutions stimulating (as they do) the development of civil society, while organized interests, the press, and others acquire skills and the inclination to make the system work well. This, like the previous item, is more a possibility than a likelihood, but it is important enough to bear watching. (Enhanced transparency in Karnataka led citizens to believe that corruption had increased, although the opposite was true.)

Giving greater attention to the wider context of macroeconomic policy

The impact of decentralization on popular views of the macroeconomic policy context is ambiguous, but on balance it is somewhat positive. Part of the time, it distracts rural dwellers from this context, but in many ways, it enhances popular awareness and understanding of it.

When power and resources are devolved onto bodies at lower levels, rural dwellers naturally focus their attention on those levels, since decisions that are made there affect their lives. This does not mean, however, that huge numbers of people shift their focus from central to lower levels. That sometimes happens, but most people had never focused on the national level (or any other sphere of government) in the first place. So in most cases, people who focus on lower level authorities are being drawn anew into political awareness, which is no bad thing. Elected representatives at lower levels usually engage bureaucrats from line ministries in disputes over the direction of policies and spending, and over the limits on spending which central governments tend to impose. In these skirmishes, lower level policy preferences tend to make at least some headway against national-level priorities. That means that in some ways, less attention than before is given to the macroeconomic context. But since pressure from lower level authorities to permit enhanced spending usually fails, such episodes simultaneously acquaint elected members of lower level authorities (and their constituents) with macroeconomic strategies.

Decentralization tends strongly to produce more transparent government which acquaints many people at lower levels with the amounts of money that are available for development, with policies higher up, and sometimes with the ways in which those policies manifest themselves in central authorities' earmarking of sums for education, health, agriculture, and the like.

Decentralization also inspires a more realistic popular understanding of what can and cannot be achieved by government—by acquainting people with, among others, spending constraints. It can also erode popular cynicism about the state, and develop a greater sense of partnership with government generally. These things tend to promote at least some tolerance for the macroeconomic policies of central governments.

Higher level authorities need to find ways of maintaining the integrity of macrolevel policies. But devices like earmarking usually suffice. Indeed, the main danger is usually not that those policies will be ignored and undermined, but that such devices will place excessive limits on the autonomy of lower level authorities. These comments lend credence to Shah's arguments that decentralization poses little threat to macroeconomic restraint (Shah, 1996; Shah, 1997). And they should reassure those who write about the "dangers of decentralization" in this sphere (see section II above, Prud'homme, 1995 and Tanzi, 1996).

Counteracting urban bias

Democratic decentralization tends quite strongly to counteract urban bias because it often provides institutional channels through which representatives of rural areas can exert considerable influence on higher levels and receive substantial resources (financial and administrative) from higher up. This is not invariably the case, however.

If it is to have that effect, the system must be structured in a way that provides rural areas with equitable or preferential representation in comparison to urban areas. This is obviously not a difficulty when a program of decentralization only empowers authorities serving rural parts, as often happens. Problems arise when individual authorities extend over both urban and rural areas.

Urban dwellers tend to be better organized and more aware and skilled politically than rural folk. This and their physical proximity to the offices of local authorities almost always give them unfair advantages in such situations. The problems are even more severe:

- When such authorities are principally focused on urban settlements, and the rural areas surrounding them benefit as a by-product rather than as the main thrust of the reforms:[7] and
- When urban voters outnumber rural voters within the area overseen by a local authority.

When decentralized authorities embrace both rural and urban areas, special provisions to combat urban bias can and should be built into the system. These might include devices to give rural dwellers greater voice, or to require authorities to commit resources generously in rural parts. But local-level councils in many countries manage to ignore such regulations so often that such devices do not guarantee fairness for the rural sector. If urban bias is a concern, the safest way to tackle it is to give rural areas their own decentralized authorities, distinct from councils in at least the larger urban centers.

Despite these problems, however, the available evidence suggests that decentralization usually helps to counteract urban bias. But this is not to say that it impinges on every aspect of urban bias. For reasons set out below, it has little impact on biased agricultural taxation which is an important element of urban bias. Such taxation policies are usually decided high up in political systems, well beyond the influence of decentralized authorities.

Alleviating poverty which mainly arises from disparities between (as opposed to within) regions or localities

This is closely related to urban bias, but it is not the same thing. Different regions within many countries, and different localities within regions, tend to vary in terms of wealth, levels of development, and access to goods and services provided by governments and market forces.

In a study which has received considerable attention, Remy Prud'homme has argued—mistakenly—that decentralization cannot help to reduce disparities between regions or localities. There are unfortunate echoes of this in the *World Development Report 1997* (World Bank, 1997a). The problem with his analysis arises from his definition of decentralization. He defines it as a system in which local governments raise all of the revenues that they spend through locally imposed taxes "without the benefit of central government transfers" (Prud'homme, 1995, pp. 201-203). He is correct in saying that in such systems, disparities between localities will not be reduced, since resource-poor localities will find it difficult to raise as much revenue as richer localities. But nearly all decentralized systems entail at least some transfers from higher levels down to decentralized bodies—as they should if there is to be any hope of decentralization working well. When that happens, higher levels of government can build in elements which provide under-resourced and previously underrepresented localities or regions with more resources than richer arenas, and which (crucially) provide representatives of such areas with the political leverage to ensure that they can acquire a fair share of resources. This is actually quite a common practice.

It is therefore more accurate to put this another way. Decentralization often facilitates redistributive policies to ease these disparities, but it is not invariably a positive force. A system such as Prud'homme posits will not ease such disparities. And an exercise in fiscal decentralization which undermines a preexisting system of redistributive transfers of resources will make things worse not better. But if redistributive mechanisms for the allotment of resources from higher levels are included, and if representatives of poorer arenas are empowered to ensure their implementation, this problem will not arise.

The key here is the empowerment of these people. Much of the literature on decentralization focuses on financial formulas or targeting devices to ensure a redistribution of resources from richer to poorer areas (for example, Shah and Qureshi, 1994, pp. xvi–xvii, xxi).[8] This is useful, but such formulas and devices are not the only or the most reliable means of achieving this.

Decentralization which is substantially democratic, and which entails some transfers of resources downward from higher levels, generates a political logic and informal practices that are usually more effective at ensuring a measure of justice for deprived localities or regions than are formal financial or administrative arrangements—

provided that such empowerment occurs. If this happens, then the creation of decentralized, democratic institutions in every area of a country tends strongly to ensure that remote or impoverished areas, or both, which had previously been poorly represented at the highest levels in the political system, gain a greater voice at those levels.

Representatives of those areas articulate their needs and press for more equitable treatment from those at the apex of the system, and if they possess substantial political clout, they will almost certainly obtain helpful responses. Evidence from Colombia, Bangladesh, and some Indian states (World Bank, 1995; Crook and Manor, 1994; Webster, 1992) indicates that these representatives succeed more effectively than was possible before decentralization. The empowerment of such representatives is necessary to counteract the (often unconscious) bias towards urban and prosperous arenas of politicians at higher levels and of bureaucrats at all levels. The empowerment of rural representatives and formal financial and administrative arrangements to promote redistribution should be seen not as alternatives, but as complementary.

Where Decentralization Has Little Promise

Alleviating poverty which arises mainly from disparities within regions and localities

If the problem is inequality within regions or localities, we need to be more cautious about the utility of decentralization—especially if it is to some extent democratic in character. It is not unusual to hear optimistic comments about such systems: "greater local participation will be important to the success of government efforts to reduce poverty further. Local government involvement in the design and implementation of (antipoverty) interventions is crucial" (Shah and Qureshi, 1994, p. xvi). But most of the empirical evidence indicates that greater local participation has tended—so far, in these young systems—either to undermine poverty alleviation or to have little positive impact upon it. (See, however, the last three paragraphs in this section.)

Why? In many political systems, parochial and elite social forces tend to have more influence at the local level—and to exercise it there in a more uncompromising, exploitative manner—than at higher levels. Even where this is not true because higher level elites have little interest in poverty alleviation, the best that can usually be hoped for is that local elites will have the same views of the poor as elites higher up.

This writer has yet to discover evidence of any case where local elites were more benevolent than those at higher levels.

In other words, democratic decentralization empowers arenas which tend to be dominated by groups less, not more, amenable to redistribution than those who dominate higher levels (Crook and Manor, 1994; Moorehead, 1991; Lund, 1993).[9] It is therefore unrealistic to expect it to contribute much to poverty alleviation where the main problem is inequity within, not between regions or localities. This does not mean that democratic decentralization is to be avoided. It has many virtues. But when it is undertaken, efforts should be made to protect poverty alleviation programs from it—by vesting control of such programs in persons at higher levels, providing of course that such persons are more enthusiastic about redistribution.

In fairness, we need to pay attention to some writings (for example, World Bank, 1995, p. 4) which call the negative view above into question. Some countervailing analyses—anchored in empirical study and not mere hope—are worth noting. The most telling of them emerge from Latin America. As antipoverty programs there have become more "demand-driven," and as democratic decentralization opens up channels which might be used by poorer groups to register their demands, real prospects for gains in poverty alleviation sometimes arise.

We must stress, however, that two crucial prerequisites for this which exist in many Latin American countries are found much less often in Africa, Asia or Eastern Europe. These are: considerable organizational strength among poorer groups at the local level, and a willingness of those groups to engage pragmatically with government institutions (Fox, 1994; Fisher, 1993).[10] If more such evidence emerges, or if poorer groups elsewhere develop greater organizational strength, we may wish to move this item into section IV, "Where Decentralization Has Modest Promise."

The second of these two ifs is a realistic possibility over the medium to long term, thanks to new opportunities provided by decentralization. We noted that decentralization catalyzes greater participation and associational activity among all sections of society. It enables rural dwellers to develop their political awareness and to learn lobbying technology and other political skills that can advance their interests. Local-level elites seize these opportunities quite quickly, and in the short run, this tends to enhance their already substantial advantage over the poor. But if poorer groups follow suit, they may eventually make significant gains too. We cannot say with any certainty that or how soon this will happen, but it is clearly a distinct possibility.

Assisting pastoralist groups

Sometimes, the poor within a locality consist in part of pastoralists. There is a strong likelihood that decentralization will fail to benefit such people—indeed, it may well make their problems worse. The main problem is that pastoralists are mobile groups. They make their living by animal herding, which requires them to move often from place to place, so that they reside in a locality only part of the time. Their prolonged absences may make it impossible for their voices to be adequately heard in decentralized democratic processes—at and between elections.

If this happens, there is a strong possibility that groups of farmers who are permanently settled on the land may take advantage of the situation to damage pastoralists' interests. They may, for example, take control of lands which the pastoralists have traditionally used for grazing—to erode grazing rights, which often tend in any case to be inadequately protected by national laws (Lane and Moorehead, 1994; Evers, 1994, p. 10).

In places where pastoralists form a significant part of the rural population, the architects of decentralization need to bear this problem in mind, and seek to build safeguards into the system. But even when they do so, actual practice on the ground may damage pastoralists' interests.

Easing the problem of excessive agricultural taxation

This section should be read as a qualification of the discussion of reducing urban bias above. Trade and pricing policies in developing countries frequently impede agricultural growth and rural development by protecting industry, setting exchange rates too high, and others (Schiff and Valdés, 1992), often to the disadvantage of poorer rural groups (Bates, 1981 and Bates, 1983).

Decentralization is unlikely to make much positive impact on this front. For less prosperous farmers, it might reduce somewhat both the cost of organization and communication, and the advantage which prosperous rural groups derive from their educational and informational status (Olson, 1971). The devolution of power onto authorities serving mainly rural arenas might enhance somewhat the capacity of rural interests to articulate their views in the wider political arena (Becker, 1983 and 1985). But the recent record suggests that such bodies will have little effect on policymakers who decide these things far away at the national level.

Reducing overall government expenditure

High-level architects of decentralization often see it as a means of reducing the overall level of government expenditure, in part because they expect it to enhance local resource mobilization. On both counts, they are usually mistaken. This misperception and the linkage between decentralization and structural adjustment initiatives (which is often made) pose a serious threat to the viability of programs of decentralization.

It needs to be understood that the inadequacies of centralized structures and commandist policies which incline many high-level leaders to undertake decentralization also produce widespread cynicism at the grass roots about government institutions and initiatives. If (as is often the case) people have also seen earlier experiments with decentralization founder, their cynicism extends more forcefully to fresh attempts to decentralize.

This means that decentralizers need to make efforts to break down that cynicism in order to give new decentralized authorities some hope of succeeding. To accomplish this, the new bodies usually require substantial injections of funds from higher levels in the early years of their existence. And given their reluctance to impose fresh taxes on an already cynical populace, they are likely to need significant resources from higher up over the longer term. This, together with other start-up costs—the need of decentralized authorities to build offices, possibly to pay newly hired bureaucrats, and to provide elected representatives with at least modest emoluments—implies that decentralization is likely to require at least a modest increase in government expenditure, not the reverse.

In several cases, high-level decentralizers have not recognized this. They have naively expected decentralized bodies to mobilize substantial resources from a heartily cynical electorate. The result—as for example, in Ghana—has been to cripple these bodies from the outset, and to scuttle any hope of the significant gains which decentralization can produce in better circumstances (Crook and Manor, 1994).

We should also pay attention to evidence from places like Nigeria which indicates that expenditure on decentralized systems tends to creep upwards over time (Gboyega, 1993). If powerful figures at higher levels in political systems are serious about decentralization—as they should be, since it can serve their interests—they need to grasp that it is dangerous to see it as a means of cost-cutting. This is true not only early in the lifetime of decentralized bodies, but over the longer term.

Note, however, that decentralization may eventually ease this problem somewhat. If rural dwellers develop a more sophisticated appreciation of the fiscal constraints which macroeconomic policymakers face, their representatives in decentralized authorities may become a little more willing to curtail their ambitions accordingly. But, since these people (like politicians everywhere) tend to fight their corner aggressively, it would be surprising if much headway were made on this front.

Mobilizing local resources

This is an important issue, worth discussing at length, since much of the recent interest in decentralization is based on the assumption that it can facilitate local resource mobilization. We need to distinguish between types of resource mobilization. It can mean the imposition and collection of taxes or both. Or it can mean the mobilization of resources other than taxes—investments in cash or in kind by people at the local level, in (for example) demand-driven rural investment funds.

Let us consider this second topic first. World Bank analysts working in Brazil and Morocco have found that carefully designed cofinancing mechanisms can succeed in inspiring significant investments of this sort at the grass roots.[11] Those successes need to be built upon, since they appear to offer greater promise than resource mobilization through taxes. What follows is a discussion of that bigger, more trouble-prone topic.

If successful experiments with decentralization are allowed to survive unmolested by central governments for extended periods—a big if since several have been extinguished—it is possible that local governments will become better able to mobilize local resources through taxation. But for the present, the great weight of the evidence indicates that they have had serious difficulty doing so in the brief period since decentralization occurred.

In some parts of the world—certainly in much of Latin America—it is appropriate to speak of "the enormous untapped fiscal potential of local government" when referring to local authorities in *urban* areas. But this study is concerned with *rural* development, and we must be careful about extending comments such as the following beyond the urban sector:

> Effective yields on most local taxes, especially property taxation, had fallen to derisory levels over the previous decades because of the failure of cadastral surveys to keep abreast with rapid urban growth, the failure to adjust tax rates in line with high rates of inflation, and widespread administrative inefficiency and corruption facilitated by the system of self assessment for local taxation (Nickson, 1995, p.12).

Let us turn to the rural sector. Some scholars argue that it is unrealistic to expect decentralized authorities in rural areas to mobilize local resources because too few resources actually exist (Therkildsen, 1994). But counter-arguments, based on careful research in poor areas of Bangladesh—a very poor country—indicate that this is not the main problem (Blair, 1989). There are, however, seven other impediments to the early mobilization of local resources by decentralized authorities in rural parts.

a) Central governments tend strongly to be reluctant to arm decentralized authorities with tax-raising powers because this can erode the influence of central politicians. (Another way of putting this is to say that democratic decentralization often occurs without adequate fiscal decentralization.) Since politicians higher up are unlikely to shed much of their jealousy of decentralized authorities, this will probably remain a serious problem.

b) Higher level governments sometimes make mistakes by expecting decentralized authorities to raise local resources without giving them adequate legal powers to do so (Parker, 1995, p. 28).

c) Decentralized authorities sometimes lack the administrative capacity to collect revenues effectively.

d) The administrative costs of collecting local taxes may be prohibitive, or nearly so (Parker, 1995, p. 28).

e) Improperly designed arrangements for revenue-sharing with decentralized authorities may, perversely, provide incentives *not* to impose taxes or to mobilize local resources in other ways (Parker, 1995, p. 28).

f) Decentralized authorities are often disinclined to impose fresh taxes, since this can undermine their popularity. This is especially true of elected bodies which are just establishing themselves, and leaders are very hesitant to alienate constituents.

g) Councillors tend to be especially reluctant to annoy prosperous groups of supporters. Yet it is precisely these supporters that possess most locally mobilizable resources.

h) Local residents are often extremely hesitant to pay taxes. They often have good reasons why, since many remember earlier, failed experiments with decentralization in which councils provided few goods and services.[12] Such failures inspire popular cynicism which can only be broken down by years of good performance by newly created institutions which do not press hard to tax local residents.

Several of these problems are often underestimated in the literature because some analysts pay greater heed to formal rules and structures than to the informal doings of politicians who implement (or sabotage) decentralized systems. There was, for example, little wrong with the formal blueprints for democratic decentralization in Ghana and Bangladesh, or for fiscal decentralization in Indonesia during the late 1980s. But the reluctance of high-level politicians to part with power created unintended practical problems of varying severity in each case. These impediments, taken together, make it unrealistic to expect great progress from decentralized authorities in mobilizing local resources in the near future.

It is important, however, to stress that over the medium or long term, there is some likelihood that this will change—to some degree. We know that when decentralization works well, it improves government responsiveness, draws society into creative partnerships with the state's decentralized institutions, makes many different types of policies more sustainable, and erodes the suspicion and even cynicism which ordinary people often feel toward government.

Insofar as such things occur, mobilizing additional resources to meet the costs of public goods should become more likely. This can occur in three ways. As suspicion of government diminishes, people should become more willing to pay taxes. Conditions should also develop that encourage greater investment in profit-making enterprises which holds some promise for eventually enhancing local revenues (World Bank, 1997a). And investments in local development funds—perhaps inspired by cofinancing initiatives from higher levels—should become more feasible. We already have evidence from the Philippines of revenues from taxes increasing because lower level authorities adapted centrally devised regulations to local particularities (de los Reyes and Jopillo, 1995, p. 88). We cannot say how much more of this may become possible, or how quickly it will occur. But it would be surprising if we saw no gains on this front, eventually.

Performing tasks off-loaded by central government

Governments often decentralize partly because they see it as a way of off-loading tasks, which they lack the resources or the inclination to perform, onto lower level bodies. In theory, this sometimes makes sense, since (as we have seen) such bodies are often able to adapt high policy to distinctive local conditions and to break down citizens' suspicions of high-level initiatives. But there are also serious dangers here.

The main problem is the tendency of central governments to transfer tasks downward without transferring adequate—or sometimes any—resources to perform them. This can result from naiveté or cynicism—two rather different motivations which often produce similar outcomes. Given the difficulties in mobilizing local resources, such actions can either cripple decentralized authorities financially or (more often) results in tasks going unperformed. Citizens who see services dry up just when new decentralized institutions are created are unlikely to respond enthusiastically to the change. The lesson is clear: higher level government must devolve sufficient resources to allow lower authorities to carry out the tasks for which they are made responsible.

Another, less acute problem can also cause trouble: bureaucratic incapacity at intermediate and local levels. This can be minimized if higher level authorities are prepared to lend advice and assistance to decentralized bodies. But what is mainly needed here is a realistic assessment by decentralizers of the administrative capabilities of lower level bodies, *before* off-loading takes place.

Promoting planning from below

High-level technocrats and politicians often expect decentralized authorities to engage in planning from below. Some analysts, who fix mainly on formalities and take seriously official documents that appear to show that the formal process is actually working, claim that this has been achieved. However, this writer's acquaintance with the informalities that lie behind these appearances raises grave doubts about whether this has occurred or can occur in most developing countries— for several reasons.

First, there is the problem of lack of administrative capacity. Elected bodies at or near the local level usually have extremely small staffs— sometimes no more than a single clerk with limited education and experience. Such employees can offer elected politicians little help with the complex process of developing a plan, or with the complicated paperwork needed to express their intentions. They also often suffer from an inadequacy of information needed to construct a plan—no taxpayers' roll, no inventory of capital resources, no assessment of the local economy, and the like.

Even where administrative resources are more plentiful—usually at intermediate levels—the process often fails to work, despite appearances to the contrary. Consider what happened in 1988 in one of the most developed districts of the Indian state of Karnataka—where the district council was served by a brilliant chief administrator with a substantial staff, where information on land holdings, and taxpayers and much else had been accurately and comprehensively computerized. On the night before the district plan was due to be submitted to higher authorities, the administrator in question telephoned a friend—a professor of economics at the local university—with a desperate plea for help in concocting a plan out of woefully incomplete and chaotically organized information that had come in from around the district. His staff were no help, because they had been trained to implement policy, and not to plan or to gather the information needed to construct a plan—a major problem in many countries. During an all-night session the two produced a plan which appeared well-considered, but the reality was very different.[13] It would be naive to expect better results in most other developing countries, where conditions are less congenial.

The problems do not end there. The elected leaders of decentralized authorities tend to understand "planning" as little more than the addition of wish lists to the annual budgeting process (see for example, de los Reyes and Jopillo, 1995, p. 88). Politicians like to keep their lists of projects open, so that items can be dropped if they prove difficult to implement or fall out of favor with constituents, and new ones can be added to please new friends. To ask them to etch their priorities in stone a year or more in advance causes them inconvenience on both fronts. Their usual response is to disregard whatever plan they have knocked together to placate higher authorities.

A further severe problem is that higher authorities who extol the virtues of planning from below often have little interest in it in practice. Decentralized authorities which submit their plans often find that they are ignored or greatly altered by higher ups. Grants from above remain heavily earmarked in ways that are inconsistent with their wishes. The great weight of evidence now available inspires grave doubts that decentralized planning can be made to work very well.

It should be stressed, however, that planning from below may improve over time. Elected representatives and interest groups may become more aware of the logic of the system, and more skilled at making it work. Civil servants who are unused to activities which support planning may become more adept at them. There is some preliminary evidence from the Philippines and Bolivia to suggest that participatory rural appraisal techniques can facilitate the planning process.[14]

But even if improvements do not materialize, inadequate or nonexistent planning from below should not be seen as a matter of serious concern. Decentralized systems have clearly worked well—in for example, India (Crook and Manor, 1994)—without effective planning from below.

Promoting community participation in development

The phrase "community participation in development" has a very specific meaning. It does not refer to the many types of participation mentioned above—voting, campaigning, lobbying, contacting power hold-ers, attending meetings, and the like. It refers to occasions when all or most of the people in a rural arena come together in a cooperative spirit and collaborate voluntarily to construct or create something. It refers to community-wide participation.

We have seen that decentralization facilitates increases in voting, lobbying, contacting, and so on. But it does not facilitate community participation in development, despite the expectations of many enthu-siasts for such efforts, for several reasons.

First, many of the authorities created through decentralization are supralocal in character—they stand above (often far above) the local level. Some of those which are located at the local level cover areas that embrace numerous villages and even towns. Such bodies find it diffi-cult to mobilize most of the population of a single village for develop-ment purposes.

Even when decentralized bodies are congruent with single villages, they face problems. People are often heartily cynical about any gov-ernment initiative. Free riders are reluctant to lend their efforts. And crucially, electoral competition for places on decentralized bodies cre-ates new divisions within villages and intensifies old ones—that is, it undermines community solidarity.

Decentralized authorities are *representative* institutions to which an exclusive few are elected. There is clear dissonance between the logic by which they operate and the communitarian logic which might inspire broadly inclusive participation in development efforts. Elections are usually won by village elites who, not surprisingly, fre-quently behave in an elitist manner thereafter.

Village societies are often inequitable, so that community spirit is limited and collective efforts tend to be seen (often rightly) as just another device for exploiting the disadvantaged. So genuine com-munity participation in development is often an impossible, naive dream. But insofar as it is possible, it is best fostered by local volun-tary associations or nongovernmental organizations, not by decen-tralized authorities. This problem should not be expected to wane over time.

Notes

1. For similar evidence from a wider array of countries, see Shah, 1997, espe-cially pages 15–17.

2. The comments in this section received strong corroboration from a set of as yet unpublished U.S. Agency for International Development investigations

during 1996–97 in a diversity of countries in Asia, Africa and Latin America where democratic decentralization has been undertaken. Discussion with Harry Blair, London, April 17, 1997.

3. This emerges from United States Agency for International Development studies of democratic decentralization in Asia, Africa and Latin America—discussion with Harry Blair, London, April 17, 1997.

4. This emerged, for example, from a talk with an enlightened champion of democratic decentralization, Dr. Kamal Siddiqui—then Secretary to the Prime Minister of Bangladesh—in Dhaka, February 2, 1993.

5. I base this on discussions with Elena Panganiban.

6. I am grateful to Neil Webster and Elena Panganiban for information on these two cases.

7. This is true, for example, in parts of Latin America and of francophone Africa. See the case of Côte d'Ivoire where many of the communes empowered in the mid-1980s were predominantly or substantially urban.

8. See for example, Shah and Qureshi (1994, pp. xvi–xvii).

9. This is corroborated by the recent research of Anand Inbanathan in India, and by the findings of several U.S. Agency for International Development teams working in various countries. I am grateful to Inbanathan and Harry Blair for this information.

10. I am also grateful to Emanuel de Kadt of Institute of Development Studies, Sussex, who has worked with the Chilean government on social policy, for information on this point.

11. Communication from Suzanne Piriou-Sall, December 5, 1996.

12.. For example, the British Broadcasting Corporation World Service reported on February 8, 1996 that township residents in South Africa are reluctant to pay taxes even to newly elected local bodies because of the cynicism instilled in them by long years of the apartheid system.

13. This is based on interviews with the two people in question in Karnataka, in April 1993.

14. I am grateful to John Gaventa and James Blackburn for information on this.

Summary

To sum up—what promise does decentralization hold for rural development? The answer, of course, depends on what we mean by "rural development." We need to break that concept down.

Does decentralization facilitate growth in the agrarian economy? On present evidence, we should expect it to have only a relatively modest role in either impeding or promoting growth. To say this is to reject the assertion in the *World Development Report 1997* that "the world is replete with examples...of decentralized institutional arrangements that have contributed to growth" (World Bank, 1997a, p. 123).

Some observers have noted that fiscal decentralization to the provinces and special economic zones of China after 1978 (which was not accompanied by democratization at that level) preceded the spectacular takeoff of growth there. This is clearly accurate. But they then go one step further, and identify fiscal decentralization as a crucial cause of the surge in growth. If that is true, it follows logically that fiscal decentralization elsewhere can be expected to produce similarly astonishing results.

There are two major problems with this argument. First, there is the question of the main cause of growth in China. The evidence strongly suggests that the lifting of suffocating state controls on entrepreneurs and, to a lesser degree, a wave of investment from outside China were the principal causes of growth. Fiscal decentralization helped, but it was far from the main engine driving the process. Indeed, policy decisions in Beijing to devolve fiscal powers to lower levels were not even the main engine driving fiscal decentralization. The main causes, here again, were the easing of state controls on private enterprise and foreign investment (that went mainly into a few provinces) which—by fueling growth at provincial and lower levels—placed massive new economic resources in the hands of political figures and others at those levels (see for example, Dearlove, 1995).

Second, we have not seen similar results from fiscal decentralization in other systems. It often helps to promote some growth and other welcome trends (Shah, 1997). But it has not produced such spectacular outcomes elsewhere because the other two main causes of China's growth surge have been absent elsewhere.

Does decentralization help rural poor or vulnerable groups such as women or minorities? Again, the evidence is ambiguous. If we are talking about the poverty which afflicts remote, underdeveloped and underrepresented subregions, then it tends to help. The creation of elected authorities within such arenas often provides vulnerable groups with a stronger voice and a fairer share of the resources distributed by the state.

The trouble is that decentralization has so far had little impact on inequalities *within* subregions or localities. This tends to be a more serious concern than inequalities *between* them. It can even make things worse, since hierarchical relations and elite biases against the poor tend in many countries to grow stronger as we move from higher levels down towards the grass roots. There is reason to expect that, over time, poorer groups may become better able to exert political leverage within democratic authorities at lower levels. But this may not occur to any adequate extent, and if it does, it will happen only very slowly.

When ethnic or other disadvantaged minorities are concentrated in particular subregions or localities, the creation of elected authorities in those arenas can assist them. But such groups often live amongst majority groups. When that is true, decentralization can make things worse—in the short run at least, and possibly longer—because prejudices against minorities again are often stronger near the local level than higher up.

Giving minorities or women special representation on elected bodies is worth attempting—provided they are elected and not nominated. But our evidence suggests that even these may do little to assist them. (This evidence, however, emerges from systems which have existed for only a few years. Over time, such arrangements may enable these groups to assert themselves more effectively.)

Do the changes in policy preferences which tend to come with decentralization improve rural development outcomes? Recall that elected decentralized authorities almost everywhere have a strong preference for small-scale construction projects. What does that imply for rural development? Opinions will vary on this. The present writer is neither an anarchist nor a good Gandhian, but he has spent enough time talking with villagers and elected members of decentralized bodies to be persuaded that this preference is, on balance, a creative tendency. Too many little things which rural dwellers see as crucial have been overlooked for too long by high-level policymakers who emphasize large-scale programs. Corrective action to attend to rural roads, wells, modest sanitation schemes, school buildings and the like is far from irrational.

Some high-level policymakers fear that decentralization will strip them of power and the capacity to achieve badly needed *big* things. They need not worry. It is unlikely that the initiatives of decentralized authorities will ever be more than just a corrective to large, macrolevel undertakings which will surely survive decentralization. If the evidence tells us anything, it is that higher-ups are not going to allow decentralized bodies to dominate the development agenda.

Decentralization can also benefit central authorities—and, more crucially here, rural development—in a host of ways, despite the limitations noted above. When fiscal, administrative, and, above all, democratic elements are combined, it can enhance the responsiveness, accountability and noncoercive capacities of government. It can mightily increase the flow of information between government and rural dwellers (in both directions, especially upward), and catalyze greater participation and associational activity at lower levels. It can improve the coordination of agents from different line ministries, counteract urban bias, and make government more flexible in its responses to local conditions.

It can bolster the legitimacy of the state and break down popular suspicions of government. It can foster more appropriate types of development, more creative partnerships between state and society, and (by giving people at lower levels a greater sense of ownership of development policies) enhance the sustainability of those policies.

In time, these things may facilitate growth—at the margins—or they may not. They may provide the poor, women and minorities with a fairer share of opportunities and resources, or they may not. But even if they fail to achieve these things, they are valuable in enough other ways to justify support for decentralization.

By identifying those things which decentralization usually does *not* do well, this study has sought to accomplish two things. First, it seeks to warn high-level policymakers about the need to protect certain types of initiatives—like programs to reduce poverty—from possible damage, at least in the near term.

Second, it seeks to lower the unrealistically high expectations of decentralization which have developed in certain quarters, lest they lead to unjustified disenchantment that could scuttle promising experiments. There are already signs of this from, predictably China specialists who share the inordinate sensitivities of Chinese leaders about threats of localism to national unity and economic development (Manor, 1986; Zhang, 1995; Oi, 1992).

We should expect more disillusioned and disillusioning criticism of decentralization from other quarters. It is inevitable. But when it arises, we need to stick firmly to the understanding—which this paper has sought to establish—that while decentralization, which combines fiscal, administrative and democratic elements, is no panacea, it has many virtues and is worth pursuing.

References

Alesina, Alberto, Vittorio Grilli, and Gian Milesi-Ferreti. 1993. *The Political Economy of Capital Controls*. National Bureau of Economic Research Working Paper 4353. Cambridge, MA.

Arnstein, S.R. 1969. "A Ladder of Citizen Participation." *American Institute of Planning Journal* (July).

Austin, Granville. 1966. The Indian Constitution: Cornerstone of a Nation. Oxford, U.K.: Clarendon Press.

Bardhan, Pranab. 1997. "Decentralised Development." The V.K. Ramaswamy Memorial Lecture, Delhi School of Economics.

Barrier, C. 1990. "Developpement Rural en Afrique de l'Ouest Soudano-Sahelienne: Premier Bilan sur l'Approche Gestio des Terroirs Villageois." *Les Cahiers de Recherche Developpement*, 25.

———1991. "Leçons des Projets de Gestion des Resources Naturelles en Milieu Rural." CCCE, Paris.

Bates, Robert. 1981. *Markets and States in Tropical Africa: The Political Bases of Agricultural Policies*. Berkeley: University of California Press.

———1983. "Patterns of Market Intervention in Agrarian Africa," *Food Policy*, 8 (November): 297–304.

Bates, Robert and Da-Hsiang Donald Lien. 1985. "A Note on Taxation, Development, and Representative Government," *Politics and Society* (1): 53–71.

Becker, Gary. 1983. "A Theory of Competition among Pressure Groups for Political Influence." *Quarterly Journal of Economics* 98 (3): 371–400.

———1985. "Public Policies, Pressure Groups and Deadweight Costs." *Journal of Public Economics* 28 (3): 329–47.

Bennett, Robert J. (ed.). 1990. *Decentralisation, Local Governments and Markets: Towards a Post-Welfare Agenda*. Oxford, U.K.: Clarendon Press.

———(ed.). 1994. *Local Government and Market Decentralisation: Experiences in Industrial, Developing and Former East Bloc Countries*. Tokyo: United Nations University Press.

Binswanger, Hans P. 1994. Simon Brandt address: "Agricultural and Rural Development: Painful Lessons." Agrekon. 33 (4): 165–174.

Binswanger, Hans P., and Klaus Deininger. 1997. "Explaining Agricultural and Agrarian Policies in Developing Countries." *Journal of Economic Literature* 35 (December): 1958–2005.

Blair, Harry. 1989. *Can Rural Development Be Financed from Below?* Dhaka.

————1995. *Assessing Democratic Decentralization: A Center for Development Information and Evaluation (CDIE) Concept Paper* . United States Agency for International Development, Washington, D.C.

Brillantes, Alex B. 1994. "Redemocratization and Decentralization in the Philippines: The Increasing Leadership Roles of Nongovernmental Organizations." *International Review of Administrative Sciences* (December): 575–86.

Brinkley, David. 1996. *Washington Goes to War.* New York: Ballantine Books.

Carvajal, Eduardo P. 1995. "Decentralization and Democracy: The New Latin American Municipality." *Revista de la Comisi 1995. "Decentralization and Democracy Review,* 55 (April): 41–54.

Chai-Anan, Samudavanija. 1991. "The Three-Dimensional State." In James Manor (ed.) *Rethinking Third World Politics.* London: Longmans.

Crook, Richard. 1991. "State, Society and Political Institutions in Côte d'Ivoire and Ghana." In James Manor (ed.) *Rethinking Third World Politics.* London: Longmans.

Crook, Richard and James Manor. 1994. *Enhancing Participation and Institutional Performance: Democratic Decentralization in South Asia and West Africa.* Overseas Development Administration, London.

Crosland, Anthony. 1956. *The Future of Socialism.* London: Jonathan Cape.

Davis, Daniel, David Hulme, and Philip Woodhouse. 1994. "Decentralization by Default: Local Governance and the View from the Village in The Gambia." *Public Administration and Development* 14: 253–69.

Dearlove, John. 1995. "Village Politics." In Robert Benewick and Paul Wingrove (eds.), *China in the 1990s.* London: Macmillan.

de Janvry, Alain. 1981. *The Agrarian Question and Reformism in Latin America.* Baltimore: Johns Hopkins University Press.

de los Reyes, Romana, and Sylvia Jopillo. 1995. *Responding to LGC Demands and Challenges: Experiences of Two Iloilo Towns.* Quezon City: Institute of Philippine Culture, Ateneo de Manila University.

de Swaan, Abram. 1988. In Care of the State: Health Care, Education and Welfare in Europe and the United States in the Modern Era. Cambridge, U.K.: Polity Press.

Dillinger, William. 1994. *Decentralization and its Implications for Urban Service Delivery.* Urban Management Progam Discussion Paper 16, World Bank, Washington, D.C.

Domenach, Jean-Marc. 1997. *Regarder la France—Essai sur le Malaise Francaise.* Paris: Perrin.

Dominguez, Jorge. I. 1986. *Cuba: Internal and International Affairs.* Beverly Hills, CA: Sage.

Drennan, William. 1995. "The Impact of Korean Local Elections." *Strategic Forum,* October.

Dukesbury, J. M. 1991. *Decentralization and Democratic Pluralism: The Role of Foreign Aid.* United States Agency for International Development/CDIE/POA, Washington, D.C.

Edwards, Sebastian. 1994. "The Political Economy of Inflation and Stabilization in Developing Countries." *Economic Development and Cultural Change,* pp. 235–66.

Edwards, Sebastian and Guido Tabellini. 1991. "Explaining Fiscal Policies and Inflation in Developing Countries." *Journal of International Money and Finance,* 10 (Supplement): S16–48.

European Bank for Reconstruction and Development. 1994. *Transition Report,* October. London.

Evers, Yvette. 1994. "Local Institutions and Natural Resource Management in the West African Sahel: Policy and Practice of 'Gestion de Terroir' in the Republic of Mali. Rural Resources, Rural Livelihoods 5, Institute for Development Policy and Management, Manchester, U.K.

Fabian, Katalin and Jeffrey Straussman. 1994. "Post-Communist Transition of Local Government in Hungary: Managing Emergency Social Aid." *Public Administration and Development,* 14: 271–80.

Faure, Yves A. 1989. "Côte d'Ivoire: Analysing the Crisis." In Donal B. Cruise O'Brien, John Dunn and Richard Rathbone (eds.), *Contemporary West African States.* Cambridge, U.K.: Cambridge University Press.

Fisher, Julie. 1993. *The Road from Rio: Sustainable Development and the Non-Governmental Movement in the Third World.* Westport, Connecticut: Praeger.

Fox, Jonathan. 1994. "Latin America's Emerging Local Politics." *Journal of Democracy* (April): 105–15.

Fuhr, Harald. n.d. *Decentralized Policies: Expenditure and Revenue Assignment Options—Is There Any Best Practice? What can we Recommend?* Latin America and Caribbean Region, Poverty Reduction and Economic Management, World Bank, Washington, D.C.

Gaventa, John. 1997. *Participation, Poverty and Social Exclusion in North and South.* Working Paper, Institute of Development Studies, University of Sussex, Brighton.

Gazaryan, Artashes and Max Jeleniewski. 1996. "Political and Economic Issues in the Re-creation of Lithuanian Local Government." In John Gibson and Philip Hanson (eds.), *Transformation from Below: Local Power and the Political Economy of Post-Communist Transitions.* Cheltenham, U.K.: Edward Elgar.

Gboyega, Alex. 1993. "Local Government Reform in Nigeria." In Philip Mawhood (ed.), *Local Government in the Third World: Experience of Decentralization in Tropical Africa,* Second edition. Africa Institute of South Africa.

Gesellschaft fûr Technische Zusammenarbeit (GTZ). 1993. *Regional Rural Development-Regional Rural Development Update: Elements of a Strategy for Implementing the Rural Regional Development Concept in a Changed Operational Context.* Eschborn, Germany.

Gibson, John, and Philip Hanson. 1996. "Decentralization and Change in Post-Communist Systems." In John Gibson and Philip Hanson (eds.), *Transformation from Below: Local Power and the Political Economy of Post-Communist Transitions.* Cheltenham: Edward Elgar.

Grindle, Marilee. 1989. *The New Political Economy: Positive Economics and Negative Politics.* Harvard Institute for International Development Discussion Paper 311, Cambridge, MA.

Haggard, Stephen and Robert Kaufman (eds.). 1992. *The Politics of Economic Adjustment: International Constraints, Distributive Conflicts, and the State.* Princeton: Princeton University Press.

Hargreaves, John D. 1979. *The End of Colonial Rule in Africa.* London: Macmillan.

Hendrickson, Paul. 1996. *The Living and the Dead.* New York: Alfred A. Knopf.

Hessling, G., and B.M. Ba. 1994. "Land Tenure and Resource Management in the Sahel—Regional Synthesis and Summary." Paper presented at the CILSS, OECD, Club du Sahel Regional Conference on Land Tenure and Decentralisation in the Sahel, January, Praia, Cape Verde.

Hobsbawm, Eric. 1994. *Age of Extremes: The Short Twentieth Century, 1914–1991.* London: Abacus.

Hoffman, Stanley. 1997. "Look Back in Anger." *New York Review of Books* (July 17): 45–50.

Huntington, Samuel. 1992. *The Third Wave: Democratization in the Late Twentieth Century.* Norman and London: University of Oklahoma Press.

Jenkins, Robert. 1997. "Democratic Adjustment: Explaining the Political Sustainability of Economic Reform in India." University of Sussex, Ph.D. thesis.

Kasfir, Nelson. 1993. "Designs and Dilemmas of African Decentralization." In Mawhood (ed.), *Local Government in the Third World: Experience of Decentralization in Tropical Africa,* Second edition. Africa Institute of South Africa.

Kothari, Rajni. 1988. *Transformation and Survival: In Search of a Humane World Order.* Delhi: Ajanta.

———1989. *Rethinking Development: In Search of Humane Alternatives.* Delhi: Ajanta.

Lane, Charles, and Richard Moorehead. 1994. *Who Should Own the Range? New Thinking on Pastoral Resource Tenure in Drylands Africa.* Pastoral Land Tenure Series 3, Drylands Programme, International Institute for Environment and Development, London.

Leach, Melissa, and Robin Mearns. 1996. *The Lie of the Land: Challenging Received Wisdom on the African Environment.* Oxford and Portsmouth, N.H.: James Currey and Heinemann.

Levi, M. 1981. "The Predatory theory of Rule." *Politics and Society:* 431–65.

Lofchie, Michael. 1994. "The New Political Economy of Africa." In David Apter and C Carl Rosberg (eds.), *Political Development and the New Realism in Sub-Saharan Africa.* Charlottesville and London: University Press of Virginia.

Lund, Christian. 1993. "Waiting for the Rural Code: Perspectives on a Land Tenure Reform in Niger." Drylands Programme Issues Paper 44, International Institute for Environment and Development, London.

Manor, James. 1979. "The Failure of Political Integration in Sri Lanka." *Journal of Commonwealth and Comparative Politics* 17 (1): 21–46.

———1981. "Party Decay and Political Crisis in India." *The Washington Quarterly* (Summer): 25–40.

———1986. "Region and Nation in China and India." Fairbank Center, Harvard University, Cambridge, MA.

———1989. *The Expedient Utopian: Bandaranaike and Ceylon.* Cambridge, UK: Cambridge University Press.

———1991 (ed.). *Rethinking Third World Politics.* London: Longmans.

———1995. *Capacity Development and the Ability to Change.* Swedish International Development Agency, Stockholm.

Mawhood, Philip (ed.). 1993. *Local Government in the Third World: Experience of Decentralization in Tropical Africa*, Second edition. Africa Institute of South Africa.

Medhi, Krongkaew. 1995. "The Political Economy of Decentralization in Thailand." In *Southeast Asian Affairs*. Institute of Southeast Asian Studies, Singapore.

Mehta, Ashok. 1978. *Report of the Committee on Panchayati Raj Institutions*. Government of India, Ministry of Agriculture and Irrigation, New Delhi.

Moore, M. P. 1997. "Death without Taxes: Aid Dependence, Democracy and State Capacity in the Fourth World." Institute of Development Studies, University of Sussex.

Moorehead, Richard. 1991. "Structural Chaos: Community and State Management of Common Property in Mali." University of Sussex, Ph.D. thesis.

Moris, Jon. 1972. "Administrative Authority and the Pattern of Effective Agricultural Administration in East Africa." *The African Review* (June).

Mulasa, Tom. 1970. "Central Government and Local Authorities." In G. Hyden and others, *Development Administration in Kenya*. Nairobi: Oxford University Press.

Muthien, Yvonne and Meshack Khosa. 1995. "The Kingdom, the Volkstaat and the New South Africa: Drawing South Africa's New Regional Boundaries." *Journal of Southern African Studies* (June): 303–22.

Nandy, Ashis (ed.). 1988. *Science, Hegemony and Violence*. Delhi: Oxford University Press.

Narayan, Deepa. 1994. *The Contribution of People's Participation: Evidence from 121 Rural Water Supplies*. United Nations Development Program-World Bank Water and Sanitation Program, Washington, D.C.

Naughton, Barry. 1995. "China's Macroeconomy in Transition." *China Quarterly* 144 (December): 1083–1104.

Nayar, Baldeve Raj. 1997. "The State and Economic Performance: Globalisation and Marginalisation in India's Shipping." *Journal of Commonwealth and Comparative Politics* (March): 20–50.

Nehru. 1960. *A Bunch of Old Letters*. Bombay: Asia Publishing House.

Nellis, John R. 1983. "Decentralization in North Africa: Problems of Policy Implementation." In G. Shabbir Cheema and Dennis Rondinelli (eds.), *Decentralization and Development: Policy Implementation in Developing Countries*. Beverly Hills, CA: Sage.

Ng'ethe, Njuguna. 1993. "The Politics of Democratization through Decentralization in Kenya." Conference paper, Institute of Commonwealth Studies, University of London.

Nickson, R. Andrew. 1995. *Local Government in Latin America*. Boulder and London: Lynne Rienner.

North, Douglass. 1981. *Structure and Change in Economic History*. New York: Norton and Company.

———1990. *Institutions, Institutional Change and Economic Performance*. Cambridge, UK: Cambridge University Press.

O'Donnell, Guillermo. 1973. *Modernization and Bureaucratic-Authoritarianism: Studies in South American Politics*. Berkeley: University of California Press.

Oi, Jean. 1992. "Fiscal Reform and the Economic Foundations of Local State Corporations in China." *World Politics* 45 (October): 99–126.

Olson, Mancur. 1971. *The Logic of Collective Action: Public Goods and the Theory of Groups*. Cambridge, Mass: Harvard University Press, 1971.

Oyugi, W. Ouma. 1993. "Local Government in Kenya: A Case of Institutional Decline." In Mawhood (ed.), *Local Government in the Third World: Experience of Decentralization in Tropical Africa*, Second edition. Africa Institute of South Africa.

Painter, Thomas M. 1991. *Approaches to Improving the Use of Natural Resources for Agriculture in Sahelian West Africa*. New York: Agriculture and Natural Resources Unit, CARE International.

———1993. "Getting It Right: Linking Concepts and Action for Improving the Use of Natural Resources in Sahelian West Africa." Drylands Programme Issues Paper 40, International Institute for Environment and Development, London.

Panganiban, Elena. 1994. "Democratic Decentralization in Contemporary Times: The New Local Government Code of the Philippines." Conference paper, Institute of Commonwealth Studies, University of London.

Parker, Andrew. 1995. "Decentralization : The Way Forward for Rural Development?" Policy Research Working Paper 1475. World Bank, Washington, D.C.

Piore, Michael, and Charles Sabel. 1984. *The Second Industrial Divide: Possibilities for Prosperity*. New York: Basic Books.

Prud'homme, Remy. 1995. "The Dangers of Decentralization." *The World Bank Research Observer* 10 (August): 210–26.

Putnam, Robert, with Robert Leonardi, and Raffaella Y. Nanetti. 1993. *Making Democracy Work: Civic Traditions in Modern Italy*. Princeton, N.J.: Princeton University Press.

Riggs, Fred Warren 1963. "Bureaucrats and Political Development: A Paradoxical View." In Joseph LaPalombara (ed.), *Bureaucracy and Political Development.* Princeton: Princeton University Press.

Robinson, Marguerite S. 1988. *Local Politics: The Law of the Fishes: Development through Political Change in Medak District, Andhra Pradesh (South India).* Delhi, New York: Oxford University Press.

Rondinelli, Dennis. 1981. "Government Decentralization in Comparative Perspective: Theory and Practice in Developing Countries." *International Review of Administrative Science.*

Ruttan, Vernon. 1984. "Integrated Rural Development Programmes: A Historical Perspective." *World Development* 12 (Aril): 393–401.

Sabel, Charles. 1997. "Constitutional Ordering in Historical Context." In Robert Boyer and J. Rogers Hollingsworth (eds.), *Contemporary Capitalism: The Embeddedness of Institutions.* Cambridge, UK and New York: Cambridge University Press.

Saich, A.J. 1993. *Discos and Dictatorship: Party-State and Society Relations in the People's Republic of China.* Leiden: Rijks Universiteit Leiden.

Schiff, Maurice and Alberto Valdés. 1992. *The Plundering of Agriculture in Developing Countries.* World Bank, Washington, D.C.

Shah, Anwar. 1996. "Quality of Governance and Fiscal Decentralization: Fine in Theory But What is the Practice?" World Bank, Washington, D.C.

———1997. *Fostering Responsive and Accountable Governance: Lessons from Decentralization Experience.* World Bank, Washington, D.C.

Shah, Anwar and Qureshi Z. 1994. *Intergovernmental Fiscal Relations in Indonesia: Issues and Reform Options.* World Bank Discussion Paper 239, Washington, D.C.

Sidel, John. 1997. "Out of Africa, Off the Hacienda: Local Bosses, Mafias, and Warlords in Southeast Asia." Paper for the Pacific Asia Project, Institute of Commonwealth Studies, University of London.

Simon, David. 1993. "Namibia's New Geopolitics." *Indicator SA* (Spring): 73–76.

Smith, Brian. 1985. *Decentralization: The Territorial Dimension of the State.* London: George Allen and Unwin.

Souza, C. 1994. "Political and Financial Decentralisation in Democratic Brazil." *Local Government Studies* (Winter): 588–609.

Tanzi, Vito. 1996. "Fiscal Federalism and Decentralization: A Review of Some Efficiency and Macroeconomic Aspects." Proceedings of the Annual World Bank Conference on Development Economics, 1995, Washington, D.C.

Tendler, Judith. 1997. *Good Government in the Tropics.* Baltimore and London: Johns Hopkins University Press.

Therkildsen, Ole. 1994. "Economic Decline and Democratic Decentralization in Rural Sub-Saharan Africa." Conference paper, Institute of Commonwealth Studies, University of London.

Tiebout, Charles. 1956. "A Pure Theory of Local Expenditure." *Journal of Political Economy* (October).

Tilly, Charles. 1992. *Coercion, Capital and European States, AD 990-1992.* Cambridge, MA and Oxford: Blackwell (revised edition).

Tordoff, William. 1994. "Decentralisation: Comparative Experience in Commonwealth Africa." *Journal of Modern African Studies*, 32 (December): 555–80.

Toulmin, Camilla. 1994. *Gestion de Terroir: Concept and Development.* UNSO, United Nations, New York.

Webster, Neil. 1992. "Panchayati Raj in West Bengal: Popular Participation for the People or the Party?" *Development and Change*, pp. 129–63.

World Bank. 1987. *World Bank Experience with Rural Development.* Operations Evaluation Department, Washington, D.C.

———1995. *Colombia Local Government Capacity: Beyond Technical Assistance.* World Bank Report 14085-C, Washington, D.C.

———1997a. *World Development Report 1997: The State in a Changing World.* New York: Oxford University Press.

———1997b. *Rural Development: From Vision to Action.* Environmentally and Socially Sustainable Development Studies and Monographs Series 12. Washington, D.C.

Wraith, Ronald. 1972. *Local Administration in West Africa.* New York: Africana Publishing Corporation.

Young, Crawford. 1994. *The African Colonial State in Comparative Perspective.* New Haven and London: Yale University Press.

Zhang, Yumei. 1995. "China: Democratization or Recentralization?" *The Pacific Review* 251–65.

Index

Abacha, Sani, 75
accountability, 50, 54, 66, 67, 92
  of institutions, 7
  to local citizens, 55
administrative decentralization, 2
administrative resources
  regional access to, 82
agriculture
Angola, 51 n14
  growth in, 117
  local policy toward, 95, 108
  productivity, 94

Bangladesh
  cooperation among ministries, 99
  decentralized institutions, 57
  democratic decentralization, 112
  earmarking funds for local projects, 100
  elections of 1985, 66
  local constituencies, 35, 75, 77
"bantustans," 85
Belgian Congo, 17
Bolivia
  local empowerment, 36
  rural development, 87
  rural planning techniques, 114
bossism, local or regional, 85
Brazil
  cofinancing, 110
  intermediate-level influences, 31
  policy initiatives, 63
British colonial elected bodies, 36, 58
  centralization, 13-15

China
  causes for fiscal growth, 117
  inadvertent decentralization, 8
  localism, threats of, 119
  macroeconomic imbalances, 68
  major policy changes, 32, 33
  redistribution of resources, 21
civil service reform, 29
civil society, 47, 88

clientelism, 66
cofinancing, 110
Colombia, 13, 89
colonial regimes, 16, 36, 58
commandist management, 23
communications, 33, 34
community-wide participation in development, 114
conditions for success, 55
construction projects, local contributions, 8
corruption, 101-102
Côte d'Ivoire, 17, 45
Cuba, 25 n6

data interpretation, 25
decentralization by default, 4, 7-8
decentralized institutions, 46, 57
  increased expenditures, 28
deconcentration, 5-7
deinstitutionalizing, 25
delegation, 5
democracy, 1-2
  at national level, 93
democratic rhetoric, 24
democratization, 30
dependency theory, 22
development projects, 94
  community participation in, 114
  large-scale, 18, 83
  small-scale, 57, 65
  local bias for, 71
devolution, 5-7
disadvantaged regions, 82
disasters, early warning, 90
discrimination, local biases, 96
district planning, 113-114
donor agencies, 29

elections, 8, 66, 75, 88
electoral systems, 8
Ershad, H.M., 75
ethnic conflict, 34
excluded groups, local election of, 77

130

LaVergne, TN USA
07 September 2010
196213LV00002B/159/A